# Powerful Presentations

**Agency for Instructional Technology**

**SOUTH-WESTERN**
**THOMSON LEARNING**

Australia • Canada • Mexico • Singapore • Spain • United Kingdom • United States

**SOUTH-WESTERN**

**THOMSON LEARNING**

*Communication 2000, 2E:* **Powerful Presentations**
by Agency for Instructional Technology

**Editor-in-Chief:**
Jack Calhoun

**Vice President/
Executive Publisher:**
Dave Shaut

**Team Leader:**
Karen Schmohe

**Executive Editor:**
Eve Lewis

**Project Manager:**
Laurie Wendell

**Executive Marketing
Manager:**
Carol Volz

**Channel Manager:**
Nancy A. Long

**Marketing Coordinator:**
Linda Kuper

**Production Editor:**
Alan Biondi

**Production Manager:**
Patricia Matthews Boies

**Technology Editor:**
Matthew McKinney

**Manufacturing
Coordinator:**
Kevin Kluck

**Developer and
Compositor:**
Agency for Instructional
Technology

**CD-ROM Developer:**
Vandalay Group, Inc.

**Printer:**
Quebecor World
Dubuque, Iowa

**Illustration, Cover and
Internal Design:**
Tippy McIntosh

ISBN: 0-538-43317-5

# HOW TO USE THIS BOOK

The updated *Communication 2000* is a multimedia communication skills series that prepares learners to meet the communication challenges of tomorrow's workplace. Twelve modules provide comprehensive coverage of workplace communication skills, along with numerous opportunities for critical thinking, project-based activities, and technology applications.

*Powerful Presentations* emphasizes the importance of developing effective presentation skills for use in the workplace. Learn to prepare and deliver a variety of presentations with credibility and confidence. Strategies for overcoming fear and involving the audience are highlighted.

The following page illustrations identify key features of this guide.

## WORKSHOPS

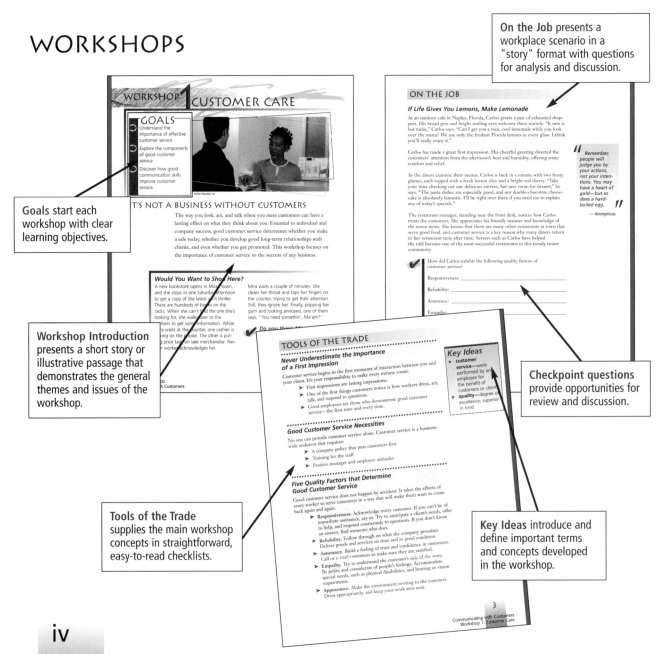

**On the Job** presents a workplace scenario in a "story" format with questions for analysis and discussion.

**Goals** start each workshop with clear learning objectives.

**Workshop Introduction** presents a short story or illustrative passage that demonstrates the general themes and issues of the workshop.

**Checkpoint questions** provide opportunities for review and discussion.

**Tools of the Trade** supplies the main workshop concepts in straightforward, easy-to-read checklists.

**Key Ideas** introduce and define important terms and concepts developed in the workshop.

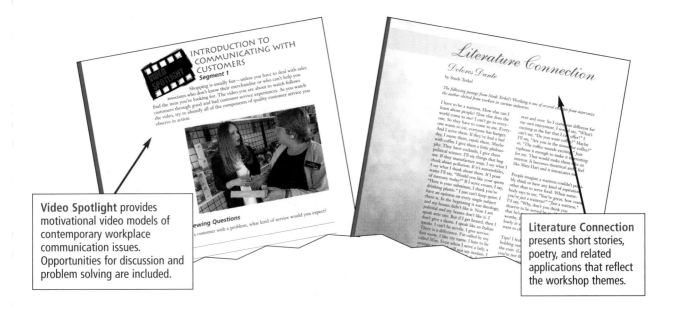

**Video Spotlight** provides motivational video models of contemporary workplace communication issues. Opportunities for discussion and problem solving are included.

**Literature Connection** presents short stories, poetry, and related applications that reflect the workshop themes.

# REVIEW AND ASSESSMENT

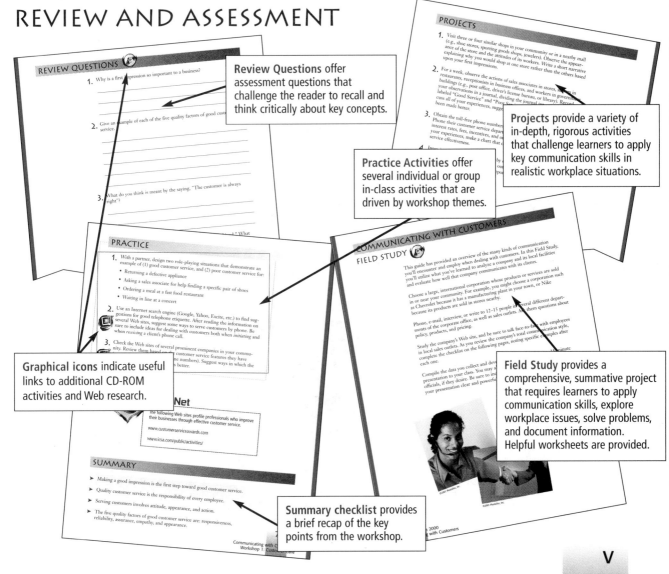

**Review Questions** offer assessment questions that challenge the reader to recall and think critically about key concepts.

**Projects** provide a variety of in-depth, rigorous activities that challenge learners to apply key communication skills in realistic workplace situations.

**Practice Activities** offer several individual or group in-class activities that are driven by workshop themes.

**Graphical icons** indicate useful links to additional CD-ROM activities and Web research.

**Field Study** provides a comprehensive, summative project that requires learners to apply communication skills, explore workplace issues, solve problems, and document information. Helpful worksheets are provided.

**Summary checklist** provides a brief recap of the key points from the workshop.

# SPECIAL FEATURES

**Did You Know?** highlights interesting facts, findings, and trends in workplace communication.

## DID YOU KNOW?

### Good Customer Service Is Good Business

◇ 65% of a company's business comes from repeat customers.

◇ Customers refer friends, who then become customers.

◇ Unhappy customers tell 8–16 people about their bad experiences.

◇ Through Internet chat rooms, an unhappy customer can now tell thousands of people!

◇ 91% of dissatisfied customers won't shop at the same store again.

◇ A company can increase profits from 25% to 100% by simply reducing the number of unhappy customers.

◇ Customer loyalty can lead to increased sales.

◇ If a problem is handled quickly and to a customer's complete satisfaction, 80% will do business with the company again.

*"Remember, people will judge you by your actions, not your intentions. You may have a heart of gold—but so does a hard-boiled egg."*

—Anonymous

**Quotations** add relevance, humor, and motivational messages.

## On the Net

The following Web sites profile professionals who improve their businesses through effective customer service.

www.customerserviceawards.com

www.icsa.com/public/activities/

**On the Net** links communication skills to Web research and online learning through suggested Web sites and activities.

**World View** provides international and multicultural examples of key workshop concepts.

**Not Quite/Got It Right** presents contrasting good and poor examples of communication skills.

Simple conventions or practices that are natural to you may be offensive to people in other countries. The following list describes just a few.

| | |
|---|---|
| **Morocco** | Holding a glass in your left hand |
| **Germany** | Being even a few minutes late for an appointment |
| **Saudi Arabia** | Wearing shorts, even for casual dress |
| **Japan** | Singling an employee out for a compliment |

**Ethics & Etiquette** requires readers to think critically about an ethical dilemma or difficult situation.

## Ethics & Etiquette

What do you do when a customer cannot afford your product but you know a competitor who sells it at a cheaper price? Should you tell the customer, discount your product, or simply say nothing?

### ⊘ Not Quite

a customer service representative for a ful sporting goods supplier. At least half of y is spent negotiating with clients on the phone.

e he was eating lunch at his desk, Luke let the phone ring several times, ller would go away. He finally picked up the phone and addressed the caller, who wanted to learn more about his company's products. Interested only in his lunch, Luke told the man that he would get back to him soon.

Two weeks passed. Luke never returned that call, but he did find out who it was—one of the biggest sporting goods retailers. When their call was never returned, they chose a competing supplier instead.

### ✓ Got It Right

As a secretary in a large construction firm, Akiko spends almost her entire day answering calls from clients, salespeople, and inspectors. It is not uncommon for her to have three or four calls coming in at one time.

When that happens, Akiko has to prioritize the most important calls. She may put three people on hold at once, but always asks for their permission first, and never leaves them on hold longer than 40 seconds. If she is not able to talk with them, she will politely take their names and numbers and call them back as soon as possible. Akiko lets no call go unanswered, which her firm's contacts greatly appreciate.

# CREDITS

## Agency for Instructional Technology

**Print and Media Production**

*Instructional Designer*
Dr. Richard Lookatch

*Senior Editor*
Lesa Petersen

*Associate Editor*
Catherine Riley

*Print Design and Composition*
Karla Dunn
David Strange

*Features Writers*
Daniel J. Crowley
Gina Mitchell

*Writers*
Sheryl Szot Gallaher
Stephanie H. Zaiser
Dr. Mark Doremus
Sandra Lookatch
Vandalay Group, Inc.

*Permissions*
Brad Bloom
Nicole Griffin

*CD-ROM and WebTutor Production*
Vandalay Group, Inc.

*ExamView Test Bank Writer*
Dr. Mark Doremus

**Video Production**
*Producer*
Dr. David Gudaitis

*Associate Producer*
Jill E. Turner

*Video Script Writer*
Bob Risher

*Video Editor*
Martin O'Neill

*Animation and Graphics*
Bill Crawford

*Assistant Video Editor*
Laura Crouch

*Stock Footage*
Brad Bloom

## Communication 2000 *Reviewers*

Anna Cook
Education and Workplace Literacy Consultant
Austin, TX

Tony Hoess
Marketing Teacher
Pendleton, KY

Carol S. Jackson
English Teacher and Technology Teacher Leader
Irmo, SC

Kay Orrell
Business Education Resource Consortium
   Project Manager
Santa Maria, CA

Nicola Pidgeon
Coordinator of Workforce Development
Schenectady, NY

Brian Sporleder
Dean of Instruction
Milwaukee, WI

# CONTENTS

©2001 PhotoDisc, Inc.

©2001 PhotoDisc, Inc.

## GOALS

➥ Understand the importance of good presentation skills in the workplace.

➥ Discover the components of effective presentations.

➥ Overcome barriers to effective presentations.

©2001 PhotoDisc, Inc.

## YOU'LL HAVE SOMETHING TO SAY

When you think of presenters, do you think of people on TV? Politicians? Salespeople? It's true that these professionals speak to groups—large and small—every day. But did you know that people in almost *every* profession make presentations? This workshop provides tools for becoming a skillful presenter on the job, identifies common types of presentations, and offers tips for overcoming barriers to effective presentations.

### Code Blue

An emergency room nurse for over 10 years, Sarah Billings felt confident when her supervisor asked her to make a presentation about nursing in the ER. The night before her presentation, Sarah searched the Internet for journal articles on recent ER advances. She made notes until she went to bed, well after midnight.

When Sarah entered the auditorium, five minutes before her 9:00 a.m. talk, she noticed that many people were already seated. She had assumed that she would address student nurses, but she recognized other staff members, some with more experience than herself. She also realized she'd left her notes at home. Sarah not only couldn't remember her research—she suddenly felt she couldn't remember a single thing about nursing!

✔ *How should Sarah have prepared for her presentation?*

# TOOLS OF THE TRADE

## Successful Presentation Basics

If making a presentation seems scary to you, you're not alone. Even some of the most skillful presenters are afraid of public speaking. Practice the following guidelines to make your presentation clear and enjoyable for your audience—and for yourself!

➤ **Plan.** Generally, the time required to plan a presentation should be twice the length of the presentation itself. If your presentation will last half an hour, spend at least an hour planning for it in advance.

➤ **Know your subject.** A presenter who has thorough knowledge of the topic is more confident, relaxed, *and* interesting.

➤ **Be yourself.** Stick to your subject, but let your personality shine through.

➤ **Practice.** Some people rehearse in front of a mirror or while taking a walk. However you do it, the more you practice, the more confident you will be.

➤ **Know the audience.** What you say and how you say it depends in part on who your audience is. For example, you would not give the same presentation about dolphins to a troop of Girl Scouts that you would to a group of marine biologists.

➤ **Involve the audience.** Listeners enjoy give-and-take. Ask for questions or volunteers, or arrange small-group activities.

➤ **Speak clearly and slowly.** Remember that the purpose of your presentation is to communicate. Don't try to impress the listeners with language they can't understand.

## Speaking Well: A Useful Skill in Every Job

When you think of public speaking, you may associate it with certain jobs. Public speaking, however, comes in a variety of forms.

➤ **Product presenters.** Salespeople and retailers demonstrate the quality and features of their products to make sales.

➤ **Business service presenters.** Hair stylists, hospital workers, and bank employees present their offerings to the public to put their businesses in the best light.

➤ **Public service presenters.** Firefighters, public health employees, and recreation workers make presentations to educate the public.

➤ **Office workers.** Office assistants, managers, human resources personnel, and computer specialists make presentations to their colleagues for on-the-job training, employee benefits, employee voluntarism, and other purposes.

---

### Key Ideas

★ **barrier**—an obstacle; something that stands in the way
★ **oral presentation**—a speech given to a group of people

---

3

## Break Down the Barriers

A little planning will go a long way toward defeating barriers to successful presentations. A few common presentation barriers—and methods for overcoming them—follow.

➤ **Personal barriers.** Barriers, such as nervousness, can be minimized by planning, preparing, rehearsing, and taking time to rest and relax before making your presentation.

➤ **Environmental barriers.** Get to know the presentation space before you talk. How will the audience best see and hear you? Can you adjust the seating? The room temperature?

➤ **Audience barriers.** Before your presentation, get to know something about who the audience is, what their interests are, and why they are attending your presentation.

## DID YOU KNOW?

Author George Jessel once said about speeches, "If you haven't struck oil in three minutes, stop boring!" In other words, you have three minutes or less to convince business audiences that you've got something interesting to say.

Those who give presentations regularly time the speech down the minute. Going through the entire presentation out loud without interruption will give the speaker a realistic idea of how long it will take.

*Generally, the time required to plan a presentation should be twice the length of the presentation itself.*

©CORBIS

# INTRODUCTION TO WORKPLACE PRESENTATIONS

## Segment 1

The ability to speak in front of others is a vital predictor of success in the workplace. In this program, you will see how presentations are used in businesses to train workers, explain new safety requirements, give progress reports, correct problems, or just congratulate people for good work. As you watch the segment, think about what it takes to be a skillful presenter.

*Kiki Stockhammer is famous for her exciting presentations.*

## Post-Viewing Questions

1. How can good presentation skills benefit employees and companies?

   _____

   _____

   _____

2. What tools would you need to be a good presenter?

   _____

   _____

   _____

### The Absent-Minded Professor

Sue Ann was a bit nervous about teaching her first college-level course. She had spent weeks preparing transparencies. She had also found the perfect video that highlighted many topics on the syllabus.

As Sue Ann prepared the television and overhead projector on the first day of class, students began to pile into the room. The room only seated thirty, but by the time everyone had arrived, forty-five students were crammed into the small room. Some sat on the floor, others in folding chairs, and some even stood.

As Sue Ann began her presentation, she knew things were not going to work out as she had hoped. Many students were hot, some did not have enough room to write, and many started to yawn. Sue Ann knew she had lost their attention already.

Which barriers did Sue Ann's planning prevent? Which did she neglect?

_____

_____

_____

_____

_____

## On the Net

How can you make your presentations less stressful? When is sharing humor with your audience appropriate? When is a long presentation *too* long? The following sites offer a wealth of information and resources on creating and delivering good presentations. Find them on the Web at:

http://powerfulpresentations.net

http://www.executive-speaker.com/kirb117.html

http://www.ualberta.ca/~pletendr/present.html

# PRACTICE

1. Search the Internet for pointers on giving effective business presentations. Combine the information from each site with what you have learned in this workshop, and create a poster of presentation tips to share with your class.

2. Use the guidelines from Tools of the Trade to prepare a one-minute presentation about a topic of your choice. Ask your classmates to offer constructive criticism of your presentation.

3. Make a list of interactive strategies a speaker can use to engage the audience. Then, ask your classmates whether or not they would enjoy these kinds of activities during a presentation. Record the responses and illustrate your findings on a graph or chart.

*Words mean more than what is set down on paper. It takes the human voice to infuse them with shades of deeper meaning.*

—Maya Angelou, writer

# SUMMARY

➤ People in almost every profession make presentations, including car salespeople, clothing retailers, hair stylists, hospital workers, firefighters, and office assistants.

➤ Giving a successful presentation requires planning, knowing your subject, being yourself, practicing, knowing your audience, involving your audience, and speaking clearly.

➤ A little planning will go a long way toward defeating barriers to successful presentations.

### *Speaking Abroad*

The global economy demands that more and more professionals give presentations abroad. What if you had to present a topic overseas, speaking to individuals in a different country? How would this be different from speaking in your native country? Though it's always important to be prepared when giving a presentation, being unprepared overseas can truly put a speaker in a bind.

Successful international presenters ask the person who invited them to speak about why the audience is attending the presentation, and what they hope to get out of it. When presenters aren't fluent in the language and customs of the country they're visiting, they must research the extent of their audience's fluency in English and become familiar with the audience's expectations and customs.

For example, does the country value punctuality? Do they practice the use of business cards? What is a respectable way to dress? Audiences appreciate presenters who express interest in and respect for their country and customs.

Mentioning something about their country, such as an interesting sight you have seen during your visit, will make an audience open and relaxed. Whatever you do, let them know you are sincerely happy to be there.

Watch your audiences carefully to make sure they are following your words, understanding your points, and are interested in what you are saying. Speak more slowly and somewhat louder than normal. Enunciate carefully, and give your audience a chance to become familiar with your speaking style. Use simple vocabulary and familiar words.

It is critical to avoid the use of your native slang. Chances are, your audience will not be familiar with it and may even take offense to something you view as harmless. Certain hand or facial gestures can also send an unintended message. The same caution must be practiced when telling jokes.

Most foreign audiences will have more difficulty understanding spoken English than written English. For this reason, it helps to present key ideas on overheads or slides. When presenting data or statistics, be careful not to overload the audience with confusing facts and figures.

1. List some ways that presentation skills can be used in the workplace.

   _____

   _____

   _____

2. List the common barriers to effective presentations, and describe ways to overcome them.

   *inexperience*

   *crowded room*

   *poor preparation*

3. Why is it important to plan your presentation?

   _____

   _____

   _____

# PROJECTS

1. Watch a session of your city council or the U.S. Congress on cable television. Choose one of the speakers to evaluate on the criteria listed in Tools of the Trade. Suggest ways that the presentation could have been improved.

2. Speakers sometimes develop inappropriate behaviors or speech patterns, such as saying "um" or "you know." For some, this is a sign of nervousness and not being able to find the right word. For others, it's simply a bad habit. As you observe or listen to a number of public speakers, in your community or on television or radio, keep track of any distracting habits they display. Be prepared to report your findings to your class.

## GOALS

➡ Understand the causes of communication apprehension.

➡ Discover strategies for overcoming the fear of public speaking.

➡ Learn how to build confidence and credibility in a presentation.

©2001 PhotoDisc, Inc.

## FIGHTING THE FEAR

Sweaty palms, butterflies in your stomach, heart knocking in your chest—you know the feeling. It's fear. Many people experience it when they have to speak in public. In fact, some very famous performers have experienced stage fright—and have overcome it. In this workshop, you will discover methods for conquering communication fears and apprehension during presentations.

### Heeeere's Johnny

Johnny Carson was the host of the *Tonight Show* for more than 20 years. Each night he would walk out from behind the velvet curtains to face a live audience—not to mention the millions of people watching from home. When he was interviewed, he admitted that he'd always had stage fright. Every time he stepped into the spotlight, his stomach was in knots.

Yet, he always seemed perfectly relaxed and confident. If his opening monologue didn't go over well, he'd make a joke at his own expense. If someone heckled him, he'd have a quick comeback on hand. In a live TV show, he never knew what to expect, but whatever happened, he seemed to be having a great time—and so did the audience.

✔ **What do you think Johnny Carson did to deal so effectively with his anxiety?**

# TOOLS OF THE TRADE

## What Your Body Tells You

Just the thought of addressing a group can cause a number of physiological symptoms of nervousness and anxiety.

- ➤ Rapid heartbeat
- ➤ Shortness of breath
- ➤ Upset stomach
- ➤ Trembling hands or legs
- ➤ Sweating
- ➤ Nausea
- ➤ Flushed cheeks
- ➤ Memory loss
- ➤ Shaking voice
- ➤ Dry mouth

## What Your Brain Tells You

The physiological signs of fear are very real, but they usually have psychological roots.

- ➤ **The judgment factor**—a fear about how the audience will evaluate your performance or a fear of being laughed at.
- ➤ **The internal factor**—a fear that you have not prepared well enough, a lack of self-confidence, or a fear of not being perfect.
- ➤ **The audience factor**—a fear that the audience is too large, has a higher status than you do, or disagrees with your opinions.

## Key Ideas

★ **apprehension**—fear of some future event
★ **anxiety**—mental uneasiness, usually having to do with some anticipated event
★ **physiological**—having to do with physical characteristics
★ **psychological**—having to do with mental characteristics

## On the Net

Do you freeze up when speaking to a large audience? Do you forget everything you've spent weeks memorizing? Does the idea of giving a presentation make you want to bolt for the door? The following Web sites offer tips and advice to help reduce anxiety about speaking in public. Check them out at:

http://www.businessknowhow.com/manage/fearspeak.htm

http://www.school-for-champions.com/speaking/fear.htm

## What You Can Do

You can overcome much of your apprehension by managing your fears and doing some simple things to prepare. You may even begin to enjoy speaking in public!

➤ Make sure that you have done the proper research and know your material well.

➤ Make sure your speech and visual aids are organized well in advance.

➤ Rehearse in front of a mirror or videotape yourself, and critique your presentation. Then, rehearse some more!

➤ Become familiar with your presentation space.

➤ Wear professional, comfortable clothing.

➤ Don't panic if something goes wrong. Just roll with the punches, and try to keep a sense of humor. Visualize yourself giving a great presentation.

➤ Breathe deeply and calmly just before your presentation.

➤ Focus on the goal of your presentation.

➤ Be yourself.

➤ Turn any remaining nervous energy into alertness and excitement about your topic.

➤ Take care of yourself. Eat properly, and get a lot of rest before your presentation.

➤ Speak from note cards. If you forget a key point, you'll have a reminder to turn to.

*Before your presentation, make sure your speech and visual aids are organized.*

©2001 PhotoDisc, Inc.

# TOASTMASTERS: DEALING WITH APPREHENSION
## *Segment 2*

Opinion polls show that public speaking is our #1 fear—even greater than the fear of death, disease, or getting fired. In this video, you will visit a Toastmasters International meeting. Toastmasters International has local clubs around the world, where professionals who make their living through public speaking meet to improve their skills. As you watch the program, think about how Toastmasters members work on overcoming their fear of public speaking.

*The supportive environment at Toastmasters helps thousands of professionals become skillful presenters.*

## Post-Viewing Questions

1. What strategies are used at Toastmasters to overcome fear?

_____

_____

_____

2. Which of these would work for you?

_____

_____

_____

## Calendar of Success

Nguyen Chan was feeling nervous about making his presentation at the employee honors banquet. His supervisor chose him to be the keynote speaker because Nguyen had received excellent evaluations from vendors and clients.

Nguyen knew he could ease his anxiety by preparing well. He completed his speech 10 days before the event, so that his information was ready. Next, he worked on his delivery. He decided to map out his preparation, day by day.

> *Have no fear of perfection— you'll never reach it.*
>
> —Salvador Dali, artist

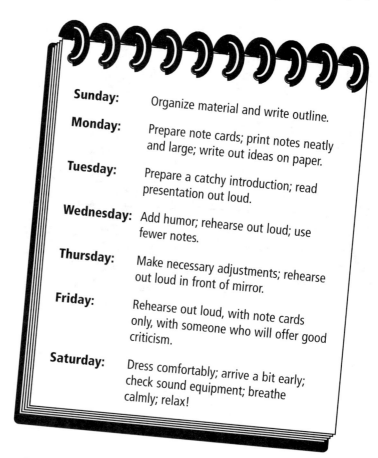

**Sunday:** Organize material and write outline.

**Monday:** Prepare note cards; print notes neatly and large; write out ideas on paper.

**Tuesday:** Prepare a catchy introduction; read presentation out loud.

**Wednesday:** Add humor; rehearse out loud; use fewer notes.

**Thursday:** Make necessary adjustments; rehearse out loud in front of mirror.

**Friday:** Rehearse out loud, with note cards only, with someone who will offer good criticism.

**Saturday:** Dress comfortably; arrive a bit early; check sound equipment; breathe calmly; relax!

When Saturday arrived, Nguyen was still a little nervous, but he was confident he'd do a good job. The audience sensed his confidence, and was behind him 100 percent!

Why do you think it is important to rehearse a presentation out loud, not just in your mind?

_____

_____

## Take a Deep Breath

Amron Rakesh got some good news—he'd graduated at the top of his class! He also got some bad news—he was being asked to speak at the graduation ceremony. Just the thought of speaking in public made his heart pound. Amron wanted to run far away as he recalled previous times when he spoke in public—his face had flushed red, he felt nauseated, and he usually forgot most of his speech.

Unfortunately, there was no way to avoid giving this speech. Amron's family was proud that he had been chosen. So, he decided to talk to the speech coach at his school to find ways to build his confidence.

Mr. Peroni, the speech coach, told Amron that it's normal to have a little anxiety. In fact, he said that Amron could use it as positive energy. Mr. Peroni also showed Amron some breathing and relaxation exercises. Amron practiced breathing deeply, holding his breath to a count of 10, and exhaling slowly. Mr. Peroni told Amron to do his breathing exercises two or three times right before he spoke. It would help his blood to circulate and his body to relax.

Finally, Mr. Peroni helped Amron to picture himself walking to the stage, standing straight, looking at the audience, and delivering a great speech. Amron visualized himself delivering an engaging opening, making comfortable and natural gestures as he related his key ideas, and then finishing with a powerful conclusion.

While he prepared his speech, Amron practiced Mr. Peroni's pointers. When the great day came, he gave an impressive and memorable speech.

 Why might anxiety have a positive effect on public speaking?

_____

_____

_____

> *It was when I found out I could make mistakes that I knew I was on to something.*
>
> —Ornette Coleman,
> jazz musician

# PRACTICE

1. Conduct research on the Internet or through other sources to find suggestions for overcoming communication apprehension. Make a list of the top five strategies you find that you believe would be of the greatest help to you. Use these strategies in your next presentation.

2. To find out more about the physiological aspects of communication apprehension, write a report about the role of adrenaline. Adrenaline is a hormone that the body secretes—it stimulates the heart and increases energy. Include diagrams or charts to make your report easier to understand.

3. Use the Internet to find out about things that people fear most. Create a pie chart that illustrates your findings.

# SUMMARY

➤ Anticipation of public speaking can cause anxiety.

➤ Preparation and planning can reduce communication apprehension.

➤ Physiological and psychological symptoms of communication apprehension can be controlled through the use of such strategies as rehearsal, organization, positive thinking, and healthy habits.

## DID YOU KNOW?

### Communication Apprehension
People tend to suffer from communication apprehension when they:
✧ Find themselves in unfamiliar situations or in front of unfamiliar people
✧ Are in the spotlight
✧ Think of past failures

# REVIEW QUESTIONS

1. Define communication apprehension.

   _____

   _____

   _____

2. Describe some factors that can lead to communication apprehension.

   _____

   _____

   _____

3. Describe some strategies that can reduce communication apprehension.

   _____

   _____

   _____

# PROJECTS

1. Read a biography of a performer such as Peter O'Toole, Kenny Rogers, Barbra Streisand, or another famous person who struggled with a fear of performing in public. Give an oral report about that person and how he or she tried to overcome the fear of performing.

2. Interview some local public officials who make presentations. Ask for pointers about reducing anxiety. Prepare a multimedia presentation that summarizes their suggestions.

3. Prepare a presentation entitled "How to Reduce Communication Apprehension." Present it to a speech class at a local school or college. Use visual aids to make your presentation lively and interesting.

4. Invite a speech coach or other public speaking expert to your class to guide you and your classmates through some typical apprehension-reducing exercises. Take notes on these strategies, and post them on screen savers on your school's computers.

## GOALS

→ Understand why effective speakers must also be good listeners.

→ Overcome barriers between speakers and listeners.

→ Learn the role audience plays in presentations.

©CORBIS

## OF THE PEOPLE, FOR THE PEOPLE

Many years ago, if an audience didn't like a play, a musical performance, or some other public show, it was considered normal for them to yell comments at the people on stage—and even throw a rotten vegetable or two! That's certainly not acceptable in today's society, but though modern audiences are more polite, they still let their feelings known. This workshop provides methods for understanding your audience's level of enjoyment, interest, and comfort during presentations.

### Give Me a Break!

An audience of 125 teachers had been sitting on hard, backless gym bleachers for an hour, listening to the school's financial reports. Afterwards, the principal immediately introduced the keynote speaker, Joe O'Hara.

Joe began with a couple of jokes and then launched into his main ideas. Meanwhile, the audience fidgeted and muttered. Some lay their heads against the walls behind them. Joe sensed their discomfort. He was losing them, so he took action.

"Okay, ladies and gentlemen! We'll take a 10-minute break," Joe said. "Everybody out! Stretch your legs. We'll get back together at 11:45." A cheer erupted from the stands, and everyone hurried out. When the presentation resumed, Joe had his listeners' undivided attention.

✔ *How can an experienced speaker detect and overcome audience apathy?*

18

# TOOLS OF THE TRADE

## Considering Your Audience

Every presentation involves give-and-take between a speaker and the audience. A presenter must not think of it as a one-way flow of information to the listeners. Neither can the audience sit passively, expecting to be informed or entertained. In order to engage your audience, you must be aware of the following elements.

➤ **Environment.** Check the size of your room, seating arrangement, lighting, sound, and temperature before the presentation. Make adjustments before the audience arrives.

➤ **Inattentiveness.** Try to regain audience interest by breaking a long presentation into shorter segments. You may use personal anecdotes to make the message more familiar. Allow the audience to discuss key points among themselves.

➤ **Appearances.** If a speaker wears inappropriate clothing, jewelry, or makeup, the audience's attention may be diverted from the message.

➤ **Audience knowledge.** Find out everything you can about your audience and their interests before the presentation. Don't make assumptions about or apply stereotypes to your audience.

## What People Don't Say Speaks Volumes

If your audience isn't speaking to you, how do you know what they are thinking and feeling? A good presenter pays attention to the audience's nonverbal communication.

➤ **Body language.** People say a lot with their posture and movements. An attentive listener is likely to sit up straight or lean forward slightly, looking at you. An interested listener may nod in agreement, but movement is minimal. Listeners who are bored often look at their watches, stare off at a corner of the room, or yawn. They may fidget or engage in unconscious habits such as drumming their fingers.

➤ **Facial expressions.** Do your listeners smile at a small joke or a good story? Do they look concerned when you relate a troubling fact or example? If your listeners don't change facial expressions, they are likely thinking about something else.

➤ **Audible expressions.** While your audience may not speak to you, they can certainly make noise! Rustling papers and whispered conversations are signs that there is an attention problem in the audience. Of course, you may also receive positive signals, such as laughter at your jokes or murmurs of agreement.

## Key Ideas

★ **communication**—an ongoing, two-way process in which a sender conveys a message and a receiver attaches meaning to it

★ **environment**—setting, surroundings

★ **nonverbal communication**—gestures, facial expressions, movements, body language, and tones of voice that convey a feeling, attitude, or message

★ **stereotype**—an oversimplified, prejudiced attitude toward certain groups of people held by other groups of people

★ **verbal communication**—the exchange of information or ideas through spoken or written words

19

# ONE OF THE CROWD

When Jay Leno began hosting the *Tonight Show* after Johnny Carson, one of the first things he did was change the format of the opening monologue. Instead of standing in the spotlight on a raised stage as Johnny had, Jay preferred to be close enough to his audience to reach out and shake their hands.

Sometimes barriers to communication between speakers and listeners are tangible. A lectern, a stage, even a balcony—all of these present a separation between the speaker and the audience. Barriers between presenters and audiences are not always so tangible, however, and good presenters must be adept at handling all of them.

 Read each of the following scenarios. Suggest how the speaker could adjust his or her presentation to overcome the barriers in each example.

- The room has no windows, the temperature is nearly 80 degrees, and 50 chairs are packed tightly together in the small space.

  **What is the barrier?** _____

  **How can it be overcome?** _____

- The audience members are talking to each other during a 90-minute introduction of a new line of clothing.

  **What is the barrier?** _____

  **How can it be overcome?** _____

- The speaker was told she would be addressing an audience of student nurses. She is surprised when 60 registered nurses enter the room.

  **What is the barrier?** _____

  **How can it be overcome?** _____

- The title of the presentation is "Retirement Ideas for the 21st Century." The audience is comprised of senior citizens. The speaker is a 25-year-old man with all black clothing, tattoos, and a pierced nose.

  **What is the barrier?** _____

  **How can it be overcome?** _____

# ON THE JOB

## Going to the Dogs

Adriana Montenegro, an apprentice dog groomer, was chosen by her boss to conduct a training session for new employees. The presentation was to last one hour and would include a demonstration of proper tools and techniques.

Adriana planned and prepared. She collected all of the instruments she would need to demonstrate clipping, trimming, shampooing, and styling. She knew exactly what she wanted to say and what she wanted her audience to learn.

On the day of the presentation, Adriana arrived early to set up and to give herself a chance to relax before the audience arrived. When they were all seated, she began.

A few minutes into her presentation, she saw confused looks on some listeners' faces, so she set aside her prepared script and began to take questions from the group. Later, when she saw some people begin to squirm in their chairs, she knew it was time for a break. When the participants returned, she had them gather into small groups to handle the tools and to try them out on model dogs.

Adriana had read the reactions of her audience and observed their nonverbal communication, and she adjusted her presentation in response to their signals.

 List the audience's nonverbal cues that indicated confusion and disinterest. Explain how Adriana kept her audience's interest in each instance.

_____

_____

_____

> **"** *I listen from within.* **"**
>
> —Thomas Edison, inventor

> **"** **Calvin:** *Sometimes when I'm talking, my words can't keep up with my thoughts. I wonder why we think faster than we speak.*
> **Hobbes:** *Probably so we can think twice.* **"**
>
> —Bill Watterson, creator of *Calvin & Hobbes*

# PRACTICE

1. With a partner, prepare a role-play in which one of you acts as the speaker and the other as the audience. Choose to explain a topic you know a lot about (e.g., clothes, pets, popular music, or a favorite hobby). As you begin your presentation, your partner should respond with nonverbal communication that tells you what he or she is feeling (e.g., bored, confused, interested, or angry). Adjust your presentation to what your partner is telling you nonverbally. Then, reverse the roles. Be prepared to discuss the impact of audience feedback.

2. Explore some Internet sites that discuss overcoming communication barriers between presenters and audiences. Make a list, describing each tip or suggestion. Then, submit them to a speech or communication teacher or to your school's counseling department for feedback.

# SUMMARY

➤ Every presentation involves give-and-take between a speaker and the audience.

➤ Speakers must adjust their presentations to the needs of their audiences.

➤ Audience feedback can influence the quality of a presentation.

➤ Check the size of your room, seating arrangement, lighting, sound, and temperature before the presentation.

➤ A good presenter pays attention to the audience's nonverbal communication.

➤ Barriers between presenters and audiences are not always tangible.

*There is no such thing on earth as an uninteresting subject; the only thing that can exist is an uninterested person.*

—G.K. Chesterton, writer

# REVIEW QUESTIONS

1. Explain why presenters must also be effective listeners.

   _____

   _____

2. What role does the audience play in a presentation?

   _____

   _____

3. List some strategies for overcoming barriers to communication between presenters and audiences.

   _____

   _____

# PROJECTS

1. Attend a public meeting (school board, parks department, Chamber of Commerce, etc.), and observe the reactions of the audience to several speakers. Record how the speakers adjust (or fail to adjust) to the audience's feedback. Summarize your observations, and present them to your class as an oral report.

2. Prepare an oral presentation on a topic of interest (e.g., food, professional sports, or travel tips) to a number of age groups. Ask teachers of several grade levels if you may give the presentation to their class. Then, try to give the same presentation at a senior citizens center. Remember to adjust your presentation according to audience feedback. Finally, write a short narrative about how the different groups responded to your presentation.

3. Interview a speaker or a trainer from a local company. Ask him or her to describe his or her most difficult presentation, most enjoyable presentation, and most boring presentation. Ask how he or she adjusted the presentation to make it more interesting for the audience. Compile the answers in a booklet entitled, "The Ups and Downs of Business Presentations."

## GOALS

- Discover the importance of knowing your audience.
- Learn how to profile an audience.
- Learn to adapt a presentation to an audience.

©2001 PhotoDisc, Inc.

## THE "WHO" OF PRESENTATIONS

If you were asked to speak to a class about math, would you give the same presentation to a sixth-grade class that you would to a group of calculus students? Of course not. A talk about decimal fractions that would be useful to sixth-graders would be old news to the calculus students. All presentations must take the audience's characteristics and needs into consideration. This workshop will show you how to prepare a presentation that does just that.

### *Walk, Don't Run?*

A famous athletic shoe company sponsored a 10K race along Chicago's lakefront. After the race, a company representative gave trophies to the top runners, and said a few words about his company's products.

He began by introducing a new shoe made specifically for walkers. "These shoes are terrific! They're designed for people who know that walking is the best exercise. Unlike running, which injures hips, knees, and ankles, walking is a low-stress activity that everyone can enjoy. I urge you to try these new walking shoes for a lifetime of safe exercise."

The runners looked at each other, puzzled. "Does he even know who he's talking to?" one asked.

✔ ***What had this business representative failed to learn about his audience?***

# TOOLS OF THE TRADE

## First Things First

Planning and preparing are important when developing a successful presentation. One of the essential parts of any presentation is knowing about your audience. If you fail to prepare for your audience, be prepared to fail!

- ➤ Identify the diversity of the audience.
- ➤ Determine what the audience already knows.
- ➤ Know how many audience members there are likely to be.
- ➤ Know how much time you have.

## Profiling Your Audience

Audience-centered presentations take into consideration the special characteristics, or profile, of the listeners. To construct a profile of your audience, consider the following points.

### WHO ARE THEY?

- ➤ **Demographics.** Are your listeners men or women? Rich or poor? What age groups and races are represented? Although you never want to stereotype your audience, your remarks will be more effective if you take demographics into account.
- ➤ **Knowledge of the topic.** Is the audience waiting to be informed, or do they have some experience with the subject? Don't talk down to experts or talk over the heads of beginners.
- ➤ **Abilities.** Are there people with hearing impairments or vision impairments in your audience? Are they proficient in English?

### WHY ARE THEY HERE?

- ➤ **Voluntary participation.** People who willingly attend a presentation are generally receptive to the speaker. However, it is still your responsibility to hold their interest.
- ➤ **Mandatory participation.** When people are required to attend a training session or a workshop, they may not feel open to the speaker. At these times, your ability to make the presentation interesting and motivating is essential.

### HOW DO THEY FEEL ABOUT THE TOPIC?

- ➤ **Agree.** When participants are in agreement with the speaker, the presentation only requires that they remain enthusiastic.
- ➤ **Disagree.** If the audience needs to be convinced of a different point of view, your persuasive powers as a speaker will be tested.

## Key Ideas

- ★ **audience**—a reading, viewing, or listening public
- ★ **demographics**—statistical characteristics of human populations
- ★ **profile**—a description of a group of people, including their demographics, interests, and concerns

25

# KNOW YOUR AUDIENCE
## *Segment 3*

Want to know about everything you *shouldn't* do when giving a presentation? Meet Barry—he'll show you. Barry is trying to persuade young adults to vote. As you view Barry's agonizing presentation, watch for his blunders, and think about how they could have been avoided.

*Barry could have given a great presentation if he'd done his homework.*

## Post-Viewing Questions

1. How did Barry spoil his presentation?

   _____

   _____

   _____

2. How would you improve Barry's presentation?

   _____

   _____

   _____

# ON THE JOB

## *Rising to the Challenge*

When Sharon Pelen took on her new role as computer trainer at the community center, she was excited by the prospect of helping people upgrade their desktop publishing skills.

After setting up a schedule of training sessions, she rearranged the computer lab so that it was attractive and inviting.

Sharon planned and prepared a motivating first lesson about how to format a newsletter, complete with text boxes, graphics, and imported clip art. She prepared handouts with complete instructions, and she duplicated an agenda of the day's topics.

When the trainees arrived for the session, they sat down and stared at the blank computer screens. "How do you turn it on?" one asked.

"I don't know. I think that's what we're going to learn," said another.

Sharon was shocked. "These people know absolutely nothing about how to use a computer," she thought. "Why didn't anyone tell me?"

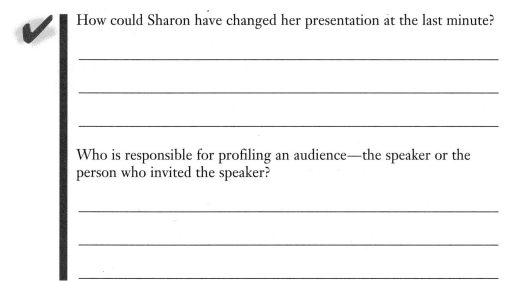

How could Sharon have changed her presentation at the last minute?

_____

_____

_____

Who is responsible for profiling an audience—the speaker or the person who invited the speaker?

_____

_____

_____

> *Speak to people about themselves, and they'll listen for hours.*
>
> —Benjamin Disraeli, diplomat

# PRACTICE

1. Speeches are sometimes sponsored by advertisers who profile the audience to determine their tastes and preferences. If you were trying to get sponsors for a speech about your town's new park, what products would be good sellers with the following audiences?

   Senior citizens _____

   Children _____

   Scouts _____

   Swim team _____

   Arts and crafts enthusiasts_____

2. Locate at least two "How-To" Internet sites—one that is geared toward adults, and another that is geared toward children. How does the presentation of information change to adapt to the audiences' knowledge? Give examples.

# SUMMARY

➤ One of the essential parts of any presentation is coming armed with knowledge about your audience.

➤ Audience-centered presentations take into consideration the special characteristics, or profile, of the listeners.

*The weather-cock on the church spire, though made of iron, would soon be broken by the storm-wind if it . . . did not understand the noble art of turning to every wind.*

—Heinrich Heine, poet

1. Why is it critical to know about an audience before a presentation?

   *top pg. 25*

2. What should a speaker know about an audience?

3. In your opinion, which audience is more challenging for presenters—mandatory listeners or listeners with little knowledge of your subject?

# PROJECTS

1. Contact a local speakers' bureau. (Bankers, engineers, doctors, or other professionals often have such groups.) Find out if they prepare different presentations for different audiences. Ask how they profile their audiences. Record their responses and compare them to the ideas from this workshop. Then, create an outline of tips for speakers, based on your findings.

2. Videotape a political speech, and show it to a group of second-graders. Then, videotape a children's program, and show it to a group of adults. Ask each group to share their reactions to the tapes. Write an editorial about the importance of adapting a topic to the audience. Use the reactions from the children and the adults to support this thesis: Presentations should be geared to specific listeners.

3. Spend an hour in a store that sells shoes, electronics, furniture, or toys. Observe how salespeople adapt their selling style to different kinds of people. Record their responses to children, senior citizens, men, women, and minorities. Prepare an audience profile based on your findings.

## GOALS

- Identify three basic purposes for speaking.
- Learn to identify and support a presentation's key ideas.
- Evaluate different sources of information and evidence.
- Use the K-W-L approach to gather information.

©2001 PhotoDisc, Inc.

## TELL ME MORE

Everyone likes to look at the sky—to gaze at fluffy clouds drifting in the blue or at the stars twinkling above. And by the time children are just a few years old, they start to ask questions when they look up. "Why is it blue? How do clouds stay up there? What are the stars?" People usually aren't satisfied with finding something attractive or entertaining. They want to *learn* something. No presentation will be truly interesting unless you have something to say. This workshop focuses on developing presentation content that is informative, relevant, clear, and appropriate.

### All Style and No Substance

Every year, Catherine Noga attends the teachers' convention in her state. Last year, she attended a session entitled "How to Manage Overcrowded Classes." The speaker was very entertaining. He told funny stories about the problems teachers have with large classes. He related humorous tales of his own teaching experiences. Pacing back and forth with his microphone, making contact with the audience, he was just like a professional comedian.

About 15 minutes into the presentation, Catherine realized that the speaker hadn't provided any strategies for dealing with overcrowded classes. The speaker was very entertaining, but what was his point?

 *Why should a speaker have a specific purpose?*

# TOOLS OF THE TRADE

## Put Your Information to the Test

No matter what source of information you choose, it should be tested for:

➤ **Relevance.** Are the facts related to your key ideas? Is the information of interest to your audience?

➤ **Timeliness.** Is the information current, or out of date? Unless you are presenting historical or biographical research, use the most recent information you can find.

➤ **Accuracy.** Would another source agree with these findings? Double-check every fact to make sure it's correct.

➤ **Reliability.** Is the source a recognized expert, or just someone expressing an opinion?

## What Is Your Purpose?

As you do your research, you will come across a great deal of interesting information, but not all of it will be related to your topic. People attend presentations, in part, to have someone summarize what they want to know, in a format that is simple, clear, and relevant. Generally, speakers choose what information to present based on one of the following purposes.

➤ **To inform.** Speakers hope to teach listeners some new information.

➤ **To persuade.** Speakers hope the audience will adopt their point of view.

➤ **To sell.** Speakers hope listeners will buy their products and services.

## Gathering Information: As Easy as K-W-L

Speakers gather information from a variety of sources as they plan and prepare. Using the K-W-L strategy will help to set the information-gathering process in motion.

➤ **K**—List what you already **KNOW** about your topic. Your own knowledge is important, because it helps you ask the right questions.

➤ **W**—Decide what you **WANT** to know. Then, you can decide where you'll need to look to find the information (the Internet, journals, periodicals, encyclopedias, or other resources).

➤ **L**—When your research is complete, summarize what you've **LEARNED**, and organize it into a clear presentation.

## Key Ideas

★ **purpose**— intention

★ **reliable**—from a source that can be counted on for accuracy

★ **inform**—to share information with others

★ **persuade**—to convince others to accept your ideas or to act in a certain way

★ **clarity**— clearness; lack of confusion

★ **evidence**— examples and data that support an idea

31

## Supporting Key Ideas

To ensure you appropriately convey your content, think of your presentation as a building. The key ideas are its foundation. The best key ideas provide the following necessary characteristics.

➤ **Clarity.** Outlining your key ideas helps your audience to immediately understand what it being said.

➤ **Simplicity.** The audience should not have to decipher the heart of your presentation. Don't include too many separate ideas.

➤ **Appropriateness.** Address your audience's interests without offending or confusing them.

➤ **Realism.** Audiences can spot a phony. Don't exaggerate—let the facts speak for themselves.

## Providing Evidence

You can't expect people to accept what you say just because you say it. Like a lawyer in court, you need to back up your ideas with evidence. Typically, speakers use four general types of evidence.

➤ **Examples.** Use case histories, real-life scenarios, and hypothetical illustrations to help your listeners visualize your ideas in concrete terms.

➤ **Statistics.** Use numbers and data to back up your statements.

➤ **Testimonies.** Use personal experiences to support your arguments. You may also bring in experts to talk about their experiences, or use expert testimonies from publications.

➤ **Comparisons.** Use comparisons to help your audience distinguish situations, ideas, and possible outcomes.

## On the Net

Powerful presentations typically include more than just the spoken word. While some speakers might deliver a polished, thorough, and compelling talk, poorly designed visuals and handouts can hinder their success. This collection of articles offers excellent advice and tips on creating colorful and effective visuals. Check it out on the Web at:

http://www.3m.com/meetingnetwork/presentations/creating.html

# KIKI STOCKHAMMER: EFFECTIVE SALES PRESENTATIONS
## Segment 4

In this program, you will visit a computer show with exhibition booths from the giants of the personal computer and graphics industries—giants like Apple Computer, Industrial Light and Magic, Intel, Macromedia, and Sony. This is the ultimate computer trade show for graphic artists, animators, and engineers. While there, you'll watch Kiki Stockhammer of Play, Inc. connect with her audience through powerful presentations.

*Kiki Stockhammer's peers call her the "Trade Show Queen."*

## Post-Viewing Questions

1. What was the purpose of Kiki's presentation?

_____

_____

_____

2. Did she use the K-W-L strategy?

_____

_____

_____

## Working Out Problems

MacKenzie Forester was asked to create a presentation for a group of new employees at the health and fitness center where she works as an aerobics instructor. The key idea of her presentation was "How to Exercise Safely." She planned to dazzle the new personnel with music, colored lights, and the latest equipment.

Somehow, the presentation took a wrong turn. MacKenzie began to talk about her experiences over the last seven years. She talked about her favorite music to work out to. Nothing in her introduction was relevant to the title of her talk.

Next, she went on to discuss some dangers of improper exercising. Some of what she said wasn't of much interest to the group, as fitness instructors had abandoned these unhealthy types of exercises many years earlier.

She went on to list statistics about aerobics injuries, and she mentioned the names of some prominent athletes and what had happened to them. Much of what she said, however, was exaggerated or not supported by facts.

Finally, she shared some information from magazine articles. These articles were not consistent with other publications her audience had read.

After receiving poor evaluations from the group, MacKenzie realized that she'd have to improve her future presentations with relevant, timely, accurate, and reliable data.

Can information be accurate without being timely? Explain, and give an example.

*No, the purpose of presentation to inform, persuade and sell. If information is not timely, you may not be able to persuade or sell.*

Can information be relevant without being reliable? Explain, and give an example.

*No. The answer is the same as previous answer.*

> *If you wouldn't write it and sign it, don't say it.*
> —Earl Wilson

# PRACTICE

1. Log onto a Web site that features speeches by famous people. Print several speeches and highlight, in one color, those statements that are designed to inform, and, in another color, those statements that are meant to persuade. Then, in one sentence, identify the key ideas of each speech.

2. Choose a topic that interests you, and use K-W-L to do the following:

   • List three things you already know about the topic.

   • Identify three things that you want to know about the topic.

   • Read articles on the Internet or in print about the topic.

   • Describe three things you have learned about the topic.

3. Next to each topic below, identify the most likely source of information. Write IN for interview, REC for recorded information (printed or oral), or EXP for your own knowledge and experience. Be prepared to defend your answers.

   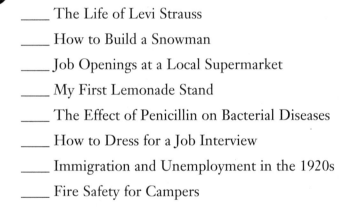

   _____ The Life of Levi Strauss

   _____ How to Build a Snowman

   _____ Job Openings at a Local Supermarket

   _____ My First Lemonade Stand

   _____ The Effect of Penicillin on Bacterial Diseases

   _____ How to Dress for a Job Interview

   _____ Immigration and Unemployment in the 1920s

   _____ Fire Safety for Campers

4. Choose one of the statements below, and use the four types of evidence to support or reject it (example, statistic, testimony, and comparison).

   • Men earn more money than women for doing similar work.

   • Children who spend much of their time watching TV tend to be aggressive.

   • Global trade enables consumers to enjoy a variety of goods and services.

   • Some professional athletes earn more income from their commercial endorsements than they do from their sport.

➤ Information used in your presentation should always be tested for relevance, timeliness, accuracy, and reliability.

➤ A good presentation should have a specific purpose supported by key ideas.

➤ Using the K-W-L approach helps speakers determine what they want to know before they present information.

➤ Information used in your presentation should be supported with evidence.

**Not Quite**

Devon is a team leader at a company that makes sophisticated acoustics equipment. To his delight, senior management has given him the opportunity to present his company's new products to a potential client in the radio business.

On the morning of his presentation, Devon puts on his most expensive suit and tie. When he arrives at his prospective clients' offices, he notices that many of the employees at his presentation are wearing jeans, sneakers, and t-shirts. Unshaken, Devon hands out very thick packets of technical information to everyone in the room, and he begins his talk. He spends more than two hours highlighting his company's latest innovations, and he methodically describes every slide in his presentation.

Near the end of his talk, Devon notices that two people have fallen asleep and another has left the room. When he asks if there are any questions, no one raises their hands.

 **Got It Right**

As a sales representative for a national printing company, Beth spends much of her time on the road talking with customers and trying to win new clients. Recently, senior management told Beth that she has been selected to present her company's newest line of printing products and services to a very large and important catalog company.

Beth has four weeks to prepare. She begins by learning every aspect of the products and services she intends to sell. But Beth doesn't stop there. She then looks at how the catalog company has used printing services in the past, what their needs are now, and how her company's newest options can service those needs.

When the day of her presentation arrives, Beth is thoroughly prepared. She talks enthusiastically about her company's newest products and impresses her prospective clients with her knowledge of their needs. Instead of trying to cover every single angle, Beth keeps her presentation to a reasonable length of time. As a result, the room is abuzz during Beth's question and answer period.

1. What are the three basic purposes of a presentation?

   *persuade, inform, to sell*

2. Why is it important to have a specific purpose for a presentation?

   *There may be a lot of information relevant to topic People come for presentation for a clear, simple relevant summary of this information*

3. Identify three sources of information for a presentation.

   *Internet, journals, periodical*

4. Briefly describe the K-W-L approach to research.

   *Know about topic, decide what you want to present summarize what you learned*

5. Describe four kinds of evidence used to support key ideas.

   *clarity, simplicity, appropriateness, realism*

# PROJECTS

1. Attend a local lecture, town meeting, museum exposition, or trade show. While listening to a presentation, take notes to summarize the content. Then, rank the presentation from 1 to 10 (10 being the best) according to accuracy, timeliness, reliability, and relevance. Write a short explanation of your rankings.

2. Use the K-W-L approach to research a topic that interests you. Identify your audience and your purpose. Then, create a multimedia presentation for your topic that is relevant, accurate, timely, and reliable.

   *Due 18 4-5 slide 3min*

3. Contact a labor union leader, and invite him or her to your class to talk about the importance of unions throughout history (or a topic of his or her own choice). Take notes during the presentation. Was there a specific purpose? Did the presentation contain sufficient evidence to support the key ideas? Was it accurate, reliable, timely, and relevant? Present your finding to the class in an oral report.

4. Interview several people who regularly make presentations (e.g., attorneys, salespeople, teachers, or corporate trainers). Ask them for tips about gathering information, how to use evidence effectively, and how to create interesting and informative content. Combine their suggestions with what you have learned in this workshop to create a brochure.

# WORKSHOP **6** ORGANIZING A PRESENTATION

## GOALS

➪ Learn strategies for organizing a presentation.

➪ Understand the importance of good introductions, transitions, and conclusions.

➪ Learn how to create an outline.

©2001 PhotoDisc, Inc.

## THE BEGINNING, THE MIDDLE, AND THE END

Imagine reading a novel by starting halfway through it, skipping to the end, going back to finish the middle, and then reading the beginning. Sound like an exercise in frustration? Just like the reader of a book, your audience wants to hear a presentation that is logical, well organized, and easy to understand. This workshop will give you some useful pointers for organizing your presentations and creating effective introductions, transitions, and conclusions.

### Why Are We Here?

Dean Martigan, a sales manager, had called a meeting. He'd been reading the company's reports, which contained the latest figures on the store's profits. The news wasn't good.

As the last sales associates arrived, Dean waved the reports at the group and said, "These facts aren't encouraging. We need to screen our vendors carefully. How are we attracting customers? Our profits have declined. We must renew our

commitment to security. And use the proper forms for buying decisions. If you have questions about that, ask Mr. Singh."

Maria Lopez, the store's top associate, turned to a colleague and whispered, "What on earth is he talking about? Why are we here?"

✔ **How does a disorganized presentation affect an audience?**

# TOOLS OF THE TRADE

## The Beginning

A good introduction can make a powerful first impression. Listeners often decide after a speaker's initial remarks whether or not to give their full attention to the presentation. Some effective ways to open a presentation follow.

➤ Begin with a story or anecdote. *(Last week, I met the richest man in town.)*

➤ Use a rhetorical question. *(What would it be like to live in a cardboard box?)*

➤ Start with a quotation. *("The only thing we have to fear is fear itself.")*

➤ Preview the ideas in your speech. *(Today I will talk to you about oil—what it is, where it is found, and how it is obtained.)*

➤ Begin with current events. *(Auto mechanics are important to our town's economy. Just today I read that people are keeping their cars longer than they used to. That means they'll need more repair work.)*

## The Middle

Transitions are like the links in a necklace—they hold everything together. To make coherent transitions from one point to another, utilize the "1-2-3" approach. When the subtopics are long, summarize each before proceeding to the next. An example, using the topic of travel, follows.

1. *"When traveling to another country, begin by applying for a passport."* (Explain how this is done.)

2. *"After you have your passport, check to see if you need any vaccinations."* (Explain the vaccination process.)

3. *"Once you have your vaccinations, make sure that you have the right wardrobe for your trip."* (Explain what kinds of clothing will be needed.)

## The End

A strong conclusion leaves a powerful impression with the audience. Effective conclusions can:

➤ Refer back to opening remarks.

➤ Include a brief summary of your presentation.

➤ Excite the listeners and call them to action.

## Key Ideas

★ **transition**—a shift or progression from one thing to another

★ **rhetorical question**—a question that does not expect an answer

★ **chrono-logical**—the order in which events should or did occur, from first event to last event

★ **topical**—according to topic

★ **spatial**—according to location

★ **causal**—related to causes and effects

## Creating an Outline

An effective presentation outline should include the following elements.

➤ **General purpose.** Decide whether your purpose is to inform, sell, or persuade.

➤ **Specific purpose.** Establish the desired effect—what you want the audience to think, feel, or do.

➤ **Key ideas.** Identify your main points. More than five key ideas will confuse the audience.

➤ **Subtopics.** List evidence, details, statistics, and other supporting information for each key idea.

Your outline can take a variety of forms. Whatever method you choose, be sure to include enough support for your main ideas.

➤ A list of points on paper

➤ Index cards with a key idea on each

➤ File folders with supporting evidence for each main point

➤ Computer files

## Choosing a Pattern

After you've developed your outline, you'll need to decide how to present your information. The pattern of organization you choose will likely depend on the topic and the type of information you want to convey.

➤ **Chronological pattern**—Arranging facts from earliest to most recent, or from fist step to last (e.g., a company's history, or how to apply for a scholarship).

➤ **Topical pattern**—Presenting several key concepts, one at a time (e.g., the costs, laws, and benefits of seat belt use).

➤ **Spatial pattern**—Arranging information by geographical description (e.g., tracking the growth of a town, identifying sales regions, or designing a new mall).

➤ **Causal pattern**—Organizing topics by explaining their causes and effects (e.g., underage drinking, dropping out of school, or fire safety measures).

➤ **Problem-solution pattern**—Presenting a persuasive argument by describing and analyzing the problem, presenting possible solutions, and suggesting ways to implement the best solutions (e.g., shortage of good day-care facilities, or a need for improved public transportation systems).

# DEVELOPING YOUR OUTLINE

Some presenters are so familiar with their topic that they forget that the audience isn't. They omit points that the audience needs to know in order to understand the presentation. The best way to avoid this pitfall is to prepare an outline—and stick to it.

 Use the template below to create an outline on the topic of your choice.

### Topic

**General purpose** _____

**Specific purpose** _____

**Key idea #1** _____

**Subtopics** _____

**Key idea #2** _____

**Subtopics** _____

**Key idea #3** _____

**Subtopics** _____

**Key idea #4** _____

**Subtopics** _____

**Key idea #5** _____

**Subtopics** _____

The best pattern of organization for this topic would be:

- ❏ Chronological
- ❏ Topical
- ❏ Spatial
- ❏ Causal
- ❏ Problem-Solution

Explain why you chose this pattern of organization.

# *Literature Connection*

## *An Overworked Elocutionist*

By Carolyn Wells

Once there was a little boy whose name was Robert Reese;
And every Friday afternoon he had to speak a piece.
So many poems thus he learned, that soon he had a store
Of recitations in his head and still kept learning more.

And now this is what happened: He was called upon one week
And totally forgot the piece he was about to speak.
His brain he cudgeled. Not a word remained within his head!
And so he spoke at random, and this is what he said:

"My beautiful, my beautiful, who standest proudly by,
It was the schooner Hesperus—the breaking waves dashed high!
Why is this Forum crowded? What means this stir in Rome?
Under a spreading chestnut tree, there is no place like home!

When freedom from her mountain height cried, 'Twinkle, little star,'
Shoot if you must this old gray head, King Henry of Navarre!
Roll on, thou deep and dark blue castled crag of Drachenfels,
My name is Norval, on the Grampian Hills, ring out, wild bells!

If you're waking, call me early, or be or not to be,
The curfew must not ring tonight! Oh, woodman, spare that tree!
Charge, Chester, charge! On, Stanley, on! And let who will be clever!
The boy stood on the burning deck, but I go on forever!"

His elocution was superb, his voice and gestures fine;
His schoolmates all applauded as he finished the last line.
"I see it doesn't matter," Robert thought, "what words I say,
So long as I declaim with oratorical display."

**How could the boy's predicament have been prevented? What does this poem say about the importance of a speech's content and organization versus the importance of the speaker's delivery of the material? Do you agree?**

"An Overworked Elocutionist," by Carolyn Wells. 1918.

# ON THE JOB

## A Killer Presentation

When Jamal Voss, an aspiring police cadet, gave his speech about the dangers of alcohol and tobacco, he began by saying, "There are two killers stalking the streets of every city in America." He chose a "shock-value" introduction, one that grabbed his listeners' attention and made them sit up and take notice.

Then, he presented his key ideas, providing evidence about the dangers of drunk drivers and second-hand smoke. He called the audience to action with a plan to attack the two problems.

Jamal easily led his listeners through the presentation with brief transitions. Using words such as "first," "next," and "in conclusion," Jamal made sure the audience could easily follow his thoughts. With more complex ideas, he used the "1-2-3" approach, summarizing an idea before moving on to the next one.

Jamal wanted to leave a powerful impression at the end of his speech. He chose to relate his last remarks to his opening. He asked, "If you had to make a decision to permit the teenage use of tobacco or alcohol . . . which killer would you choose?"

> *If you can't write your message in a sentence, you can't say it in an hour.*
>
> —Diana Booher, motivational speaker

✔ Why is a good introduction important to a presentation?

*A good introduction makes a powerful impression.*

©2001 PhotoDisc, Inc.

*Your audience wants to hear a presentation that is logical, well organized, and easy to understand.*


43

Powerful Presentations
Workshop 6: Organizing a Presentation

# PRACTICE

1. Label each topic below with the most appropriate pattern of organization. Write CH for chronological, SP for spatial, TO for topical, CA for causal, and PS for problem-solution. Use each response twice, and be prepared to defend your answers.

   _SP_ Designing a New Stadium

   ____ Polio and Other Diseases

   ____ The Writings of Frederick Douglass

   ____ Manufacturing Steel

   ____ Ending Global Warming

   ____ The Life of Jane Addams

   ____ Electronic Banking

   _SP_ How to Install Computer Software

   _CA_ Why Teens Smoke

   _CH_ Twentieth Century Immigration

2. Using the techniques described in this workshop, work with a partner to write a strong introduction and conclusion about the topic of your choice.

3. Use the Internet or other sources to find and read an informative or persuasive speech. Identify and analyze its introduction, purpose, key ideas, subtopics, and conclusion. Write an evaluation of the speech based on what you have learned in this workshop.

# SUMMARY

➤ Presentations should be logical, well organized, and easy to understand.

➤ Outlining is an effective method for organizing a presentation.

➤ A strong introduction, appropriate transitions, and a powerful conclusion can strengthen the impact of a presentation.

# REVIEW QUESTIONS

1. List and describe five common patterns for organizing presentations.

   _Chronological pattern - arranging fact from earliest to most; topical pattern_

2. Why is the organization of a presentation critical to its success?

3. Identify some strategies for developing good introductions, transitions, and conclusions.

# PROJECTS

1. Television commercials can be seen as short presentations. They begin with an introduction, guide viewers through key ideas, and end with a conclusion. Videotape several commercials, analyze them, and create outlines of their introductions, transitions, key ideas, and conclusions. Then, show the commercials in class, and explain your analyses.

2. Collect four or five magazine articles about the same topic. Compare their introductions, key ideas, transitions, and conclusions. Prepare an oral report evaluating the quality of each article. Choose one article, and create an outline for it.

3. Locate several Web sites that provide tips for organizing a presentation. Combine the tips with what you have learned in this workshop to produce a multimedia presentation outlining and explaining "How to Organize a Presentation."

# WORKSHOP 7 INVOLVING THE AUDIENCE

## GOALS

- Learn how to involve an audience in a presentation.
- Understand the role of visual aids.
- Identify and assess different types of visual aids.

©2001 PhotoDisc, Inc.

## DRAWING IN YOUR LISTENERS

No group is more difficult to engage than a captive audience—one that is forced to attend a presentation. Yet some people win over their captive listeners, every day, and do it very well. You have probably had instructors who made their lessons lively and fun, despite students' mandatory attendance. How do they do it? By involving you—the audience. This workshop demonstrates the importance of involving the audience during presentations, provides techniques for drawing in the audience, and describes effective uses of visual aids.

### Making It Real

Alcohol-related traffic deaths and underage drinking are on the rise. In an attempt to reverse this dangerous trend, two speakers—both recovering alcoholics—recently presented information to a traffic school.

The first speaker stood at the front of the room and listed statistics about the numbers of incidents in different cities. Then he talked about the effects on victims.

The second speaker vividly recounted his past experiences. He talked about the night he caused a horrible accident, and about his slow, painful recovery. He finished his presentation by asking, "Do you want to end up like I did?"

 ***Which speaker caught the audience's attention? Why?***

# TOOLS OF THE TRADE

## Involving the Audience

The best techniques for involving an audience are those that are realistic and genuine, such as stories from personal experience, case studies about actual people and events, and humorous anecdotes. To engage the audience, skillful presenters must also consider their listeners' emotions, values, and beliefs.

➤ **Establish common ground.** A speaker talking to a group of soccer coaches might relate something about his or her own soccer-playing experiences.

➤ **Appeal to beliefs and values.** A speaker trying to convince a group of people who do not have school-age children to vote for building a new school might appeal to the group's concerns for public safety by focusing on the fact that having good schools reduces crime rates.

➤ **Engage the listeners.** A speaker wanting to motivate listeners to donate money for disaster victims might use descriptive, emotional language to illustrate the devastation of a tornado or an earthquake.

## Picture This

Most successful presentations include visual aids. These may be charts, graphs, pictures, diagrams, models, or slides. Visual aids must suit the needs of both the audience and the topic. When you are selecting visual aids, always be aware of who your audience will be.

| What Good Visual Aids Do | Examples |
|---|---|
| Clarify meaning | Outline of key ideas<br>Map<br>Diagram |
| Increase authority | Product examples<br>Demonstrations<br>Outline with quotes<br>Videos of experts |
| Sustain audience interest | A series of before-and-after photos<br>Recordings<br>Guest speakers |
| Help audiences learn and retain information | Lists of examples<br>Repeated words and phrases |

## Key Ideas

★ **visual aid—** something such as a model, chart, or movie that is used as a complement to a lesson or presentation

★ **anecdote—** a brief story that is amusing, interesting, or personal

★ **value—**to have a high regard for someone or something

★ **transparency—** a sheet of plastic used to show images with a projector

★ **graphic—** a visual device, such as a chart, a photo, or a map that is used to illustrate information

## Look Them in the Eye

If an audience is small, you can maintain eye contact by focusing on one person at a time. It's not as easy when your audience is large, but here are some tips that will help you to be engaged with the whole group.

➤ Establish eye contact with the people at the back of the room first.

➤ Maintain eye contact for three to five seconds.

➤ If you cannot see your listeners' eyes, focus on their faces.

➤ Shift your gaze from one part of the audience to another.

## Designing Visual Aids

When you prepare visual aids, remember that communicating your message is your main goal. If the print on your visual aids is too small or too cluttered, the audience will miss your point.

➤ The bigger the room, the bigger your type should be.

➤ Present only one or two ideas on each slide or transparency.

➤ Don't use more than seven lines, and don't use more than seven words per line.

➤ Leave plenty of white space.

➤ Neatness counts.

➤ Use simple phrases, diagrams, and illustrations.

➤ Remember the KISS technique: Keep It Short and Simple.

## Slide Show Presentations

An effective computer slide show can enhance a presentation with authentic photos, sound, and video. Poorly designed slides can be a distraction, however. Keep the following points in mind.

➤ Graphics should be big and bold; do not use more than two per slide.

➤ Arrange the slides so that there is space between lines of text.

➤ Include your company's logo on each slide and stick with the same colors and size throughout the show.

➤ Use contrasting colors; dark backgrounds with light text are good, but don't overdo it.

➤ Use an easily read font size between 18 pt. and 48 pt., and use a maximum of two fonts per slide.

➤ Avoid using all capital letters or abbreviations in text.

➤ If you have access to a laser light, use it only sparingly.

# AIRWALK: INVOLVING THE AUDIENCE
## Segment 5

In this program, you will visit airwalk, a producer of popular skating, snow, and bike gear, as they kick off their annual sales meeting. This meeting provides airwalk's salespeople with valuable information about airwalk's new products. During the program, you'll witness what goes into developing presentation strategies for airwalk's sales meeting. As you watch the event, think about the strategies airwalk uses to involve the audience.

*Andrew Shaddy talks about airwalk's new products.*

## Post-Viewing Questions

1. How does Andrew Shaddy involve the audience?

   _____

   _____

   _____

2. What makes audience participation so important to airwalk?

   _____

   _____

   _____

# *Literature Connection*

## *excerpt from I Have a Dream*

By Dr. Martin Luther King, Jr.

*King's famous speech was delivered August 28, 1963 at the March on Washington, in front of more than 200,000 people assembled at the Lincoln Memorial.*

I say to you today, my friends, even though we face the difficulties of today and tomorrow, I still have a dream. It is a dream deeply rooted in the American dream. I have a dream that one day this nation will rise up and live out the true meaning of its creed, "We hold these truths to be self-evident; that all men are created equal." I have a dream that one day on the red hills of Georgia, sons of former slaves and the sons of former slave owners will be able to sit down together at the table of brotherhood. I have a dream that one day even the state of Mississippi, a state sweltering with the heat of injustice, sweltering with the heat of oppression, will be transformed into an oasis of freedom and justice. I have a dream that my four little children will one day live in a nation where they will not be judged by the color of their skin, but by the content of their character.

I have a dream today!

I have a dream that one day down in Alabama—with its vicious racists, with its Governor having his lips dripping with the words of interposition and nullification—one day right there in Alabama, little black boys and black girls will be able to join hands with little white boys and white girls as sisters and brothers.

I have a dream today!

I have a dream that one day every valley shall be exalted, and every hill and mountain shall be made low. The rough places will be plain and the crooked places will be made straight, "and the glory of the Lord shall be revealed, and all flesh shall see it together."

This is our hope. This is the faith that I go back to the South with. With this faith we will be able to hew out of the mountain of despair a stone of hope. With this faith we will be able to transform the jangling discords of our nation into a beautiful symphony of brotherhood. With this faith we will be able to work together, to pray together, to struggle together, to go to jail together, to stand up for freedom together, knowing that we will be free one day. And this will be the day. This will be the day when all of God's children will be able to sing with new meaning, "My country 'tis of thee, sweet land of liberty, of thee I sing. Land where my fathers died, land of the pilgrims' pride, from every mountainside, let freedom ring." And if America is to be a great nation, this must become true.

So let freedom ring from the prodigious hilltops of New Hampshire; let freedom ring from the mighty mountains of New York; let freedom ring from the heightening Alleghenies of Pennsylvania; let freedom ring from the snow-capped Rockies of Colorado; let freedom ring from the curvaceous slopes of California. But not only that. Let freedom ring from Stone Mountain of Georgia; let freedom ring from Lookout Mountain of Tennessee; let freedom ring from every hill and molehill of Mississippi. "From every mountainside, let freedom ring."

And when this happens, and when we allow freedom to ring, when we let it ring from every village and every hamlet, from every state and every city, we will be able to speed up that day when all of God's children—black men and white men, Jews and Gentiles, Protestants and Catholics—will be able to join hands and sing in the words of the old Negro spiritual, "Free at last. Free at last. Thank God Almighty, we are free at last."

**In this famous speech, how does King 1) establish common ground with his audience, 2) appeal to his audience's beliefs and values, and 3) engage his listeners? Give examples from the speech to support your answers.**

# DON'T JUST TELL ME, SHOW ME

Many people wouldn't expect a lecture on electronic banking to be very exciting. Those people probably don't know Jeff Siegel, an economist with the Federal Reserve Bank of Chicago. Not only does Jeff know his economics, he's an innovative speaker who knows how to captivate an audience.

Jeff begins his presentation—"The Good, the Bad, and the Ugly"—with the soundtrack from a famous Clint Eastwood movie—complete with a close-up of Clint murmuring, "Go ahead, make my day." Jeff's talk is about the *good* features of ATMs and bank cards, the *bad* things that can happen if people are careless with confidential information, and the *ugly* effects that poor security can have on your credit report. Though Jeff could deliver his message with nothing more than a blackboard and a piece of chalk, he makes dull material lively through the use of stories, cartoons, live images, and sound effects.

 Think of a visual aid you could use to enhance each topic below. Then, write a short example of how you would use the visual aid to engage your audience. Be creative!

- Preparing for a Job Interview

- Car Buying: Lease or Own?

- Furnishing Your First Apartment

- Caring for a New Baby

- A Dream Vacation to Europe

- Which Computer Should I Buy?

- How to Quit Smoking

- Hit Music of the '70s and '80s

- Should I Start My Own Business?

- Advantages of Speaking a Second Language

> *The eloquent man is he who is no beautiful speaker, but who is inwardly and desperately drunk with a certain belief.*
>
> —Ralph Waldo Emerson, writer

# ON THE JOB

## All of His Eggs in One Basket

Gironis Carroll, a sales executive, had prepared a high-tech computer show for a two-hour presentation at a big toy convention. He used animation, sound, recorded voices, streaming video, and full-color charts and graphs. He was sure that this vivid and entertaining presentation would bring in many sales for his company's new product line.

Gironis arrived early to set up the projector for his computer and to test the power sources. He also checked out the view from every part of the room. "Everything looks great!" he thought confidently. "This is going to be one terrific presentation."

By 9:30, the room was filled with buyers waiting to see the latest from this company's innovators. Gironis clicked his remote control to begin the show— and his worst nightmare began to come true. His laptop displayed the awful words: "Disk error. Unable to access program."

Gironis nearly panicked as he tried in vain to load the program. After 10 minutes, it was obvious that he would have to do something else. But what would he talk about for two hours without his visuals? Gironis had made a huge mistake. His visuals did not just add to his presentation—they *were* his presentation.

 What are some ways you could continue a presentation about sightseeing in Paris if your slide projector failed?

_____

_____

# On the Net

One of the most popular presentation graphics programs, Microsoft PowerPoint, is just one of the tools professional presenters use to involve their audiences and help organize their ideas. Learn more about this program and its many features, including how to add animation and sound to your presentation slides at:

http://www.microsoft.com/powerpointdev/p-tips.htm

# PRACTICE

1. For each of the following, suggest a visual aid that would help an audience gain a better understanding of the topic.

How to plant a tree _____

Adding fractions _____

Reading a train schedule _____

Highlights of a trip to Alaska _____

Advantages and disadvantages of drinking diet beverages _____

Top five reasons for learning to play the piano _____

2. Look at some Internet auction Web sites, and describe the visual aids used to attract customers. Suggest alternative visual aids for at least three products. Visuals may include banners, icons, photographs, navigation buttons, and logos.

> " *No man for any considerable period can wear one face to himself and another to the multitude, without finally getting bewildered as to which may be the true.* "
>
> —Nathaniel Hawthorne, writer

# SUMMARY

➤ Engaging an audience is an essential component of any presentation.

➤ To engage the audience, skillful presenters must consider their listeners' emotions, values, and beliefs.

➤ When used appropriately, visual aids can enhance a presentation.

# REVIEW QUESTIONS

1. Explain some strategies for involving an audience in a presentation.

   _____

   _____

   _____

   _____

2. Describe several kinds of visual aids, and explain how they can be used most effectively.

   _____

   _____

   _____

   _____

# PROJECTS

1. Watch an infomercial (a show that resembles a television program but is actually a 30-minute or 60-minute commercial for a product). List all the techniques that the host(s) used to engage the audience. Also list their visual aids. Finally, write an analysis of the effectiveness of the presentation techniques and visual aids, and recommend other visual aids to increase audience involvement.

2. Tape a five-minute news broadcast on the radio. Replay it a few times, and think of some visual aids that could enhance the individual news stories. Create these visual aids, and display them to your class while you replay the taped broadcast. Have members of your class evaluate how the visuals enhanced the broadcast.

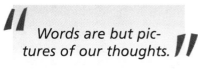

*Words are but pictures of our thoughts.*

—John Dryden, poet

# 8 QUESTIONS AND ANSWERS

©CORBIS

## BEGGING THE QUESTIONS

At most music concerts, the crowd yells, "Encore!" until the musicians return to play a few more crowd favorites. Musicians know that audience members particularly like the chance to make some special requests. In a presentation, questions and discussions are like encores—they give the audience a chance to interact. This workshop presents methods for managing successful discussions and Q & A sessions during your presentation.

### Hot Air

Karen Briard has worked within the same university department for six years. Each year, she attends a mandatory meeting on workplace safety. Karen is very conscientious about health and safety, and finds that she usually remembers most of what she had learned at the previous year's meeting.

This year, however, there was something new. Volunteers from the campus fire department came to demonstrate how to use the building's fire extinguishers, fire hoses, and fire hydrants. They explained the procedures and then hurriedly left for another demonstration. After the firefighters left, Karen wasn't sure she remembered which extinguishers to use with what types of fires, and she wasn't sure she could operate one of them, let alone a fire hose.

✔ **What was wrong with the firefighters' demonstration?**

# TOOLS OF THE TRADE

## Before Your Presentation: Anticipating Questions

Holiday Inn's advertising slogan once was, "The best surprise is no surprise." When you're giving a presentation, there is nothing more challenging than handling a surprise question. Your presentation isn't ready until you feel confident about taking questions from your audience.

➤ **Research your topic.** If you learn more than what you actually plan to present, you will be more confident about answering questions.

➤ **Anticipate questions.** Practice your presentation with some friends. When you're finished, have your friends to ask difficult questions. Make note of any questions you need to do more research to answer.

➤ **Plan how you will take questions.** Will you allow the audience to interrupt your talk? Will you take questions at the end? Will you allow some people to stay after your presentation to ask you questions individually? Each method for taking questions has advantages and disadvantages.

| METHOD | ADVANTAGES | DISADVANTAGES |
|---|---|---|
| **Allowing the audience to interrupt.** | Instant explanations of ideas. | Speaker may lose focus. |
| **Taking questions at the end.** | Speaker can conclude remarks without interruption. | Less spontaneous. |
| **Talking with individuals afterward.** | Allows speaker to network with the audience and permits the audience to ask all of their questions. | Less assertive participants may not be heard. |

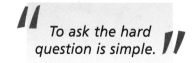

*To ask the hard question is simple.*

—W.H. Auden, poet

## During Your Presentation: Handling Questions

A successful Q & A session requires more than anticipating questions and planning answers. The following pointers will help to make your Q & A session structured, pleasant, and professional.

➤ Ask people to stand when asking their questions so that everyone can hear them.

➤ Provide paper so that your listeners can jot down questions while you speak. Some people are also more comfortable if you collect questions and read them aloud, so that they will not have to stand up in front of a group.

➤ Look directly at your questioner.

➤ Listen carefully to the entire question before answering.

➤ Restate the question so that everyone hears it and so that you have time to think.

➤ Answer honestly. It's all right to say, "I don't know." Tell the questioner you will find the information and get back to them—and then do so.

➤ Defuse rude or confrontational audience members by rephrasing negative questions and handling attacks with good humor.

➤ Stop long-winded questioners politely, and offer to discuss irrelevant questions after the presentation.

*Your presentation isn't ready until you feel confident about taking questions from your audience.*

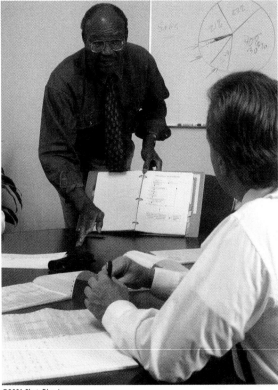

©2001 PhotoDisc, Inc.

# EVALUATING YOUR Q & A

American actress Shirley Booth once said, "The audience is 50 percent of the performance." Involving your listeners with a controlled approach is probably 100 percent of managing your Q & A session. For example, musical performers rely on the structured nature of encores. When audiences know in advance that their chance to participate will come, performers deal with fewer shouted requests and interruptions from the crowd. Stand-up comedians, however, have no structured format for involving the audience. They must constantly deal with hecklers—audience members who deliberately interrupt by shouting rude or funny comments. Providing a structured environment for questions and dealing with unwelcome interruptions is your job as the presenter.

Working with a partner, choose two different news articles or editorials from a local newspaper or national magazine. Each person should read one article and anticipate questions that an audience might ask. The first speaker should summarize the article orally for his or her partner (the listener), who then creates at least five questions about the presentation. Make sure to give the speaker practice with defusing irrelevant or long-winded questions. After the speaker responds to the questions, the listener should rank those responses using the form below. Then, switch roles and repeat the exercise.

## Q & A Evaluation

|  | Excellent | Good | Fair | Poor |
|---|---|---|---|---|
| Looked at the questioner | 4 | 3 | 2 | 1 |
| Listened carefully to the question | 4 | 3 | 2 | 1 |
| Restated the question | 4 | 3 | 2 | 1 |
| Paused before answering | 4 | 3 | 2 | 1 |
| Responded honestly and thoroughly | 4 | 3 | 2 | 1 |
| Rephrased negative questions | 4 | 3 | 2 | 1 |
| Stopped long-winded questions politely | 4 | 3 | 2 | 1 |
| Defused irrelevant questions | 4 | 3 | 2 | 1 |

### Put on a Happy Face

When Serena Greenfield was asked to speak about workplace competencies at a seminar for recent college graduates, she planned to cover the topics of work ethics and communication skills. During her presentation, she was interrupted by a participant who began to tell horror stories about his first job. He felt that he had been discriminated against in various companies, and he complained that he'd experienced difficulty in relocating and finding suitable work.

Serena could see that the audience was becoming annoyed by how this questioner was taking over the discussion. She also knew that if she were rude, she would lose her credibility as a presenter.

"I understand your frustrations, sir," she said graciously. "The workplace can sometimes seem unfair. I would like to talk with you at length about your work experiences. We'll be taking a break in a few minutes, and we can talk about it then if you like. In the meanwhile, I'd like to distribute these handouts so that we can move on to the next topic."

Serena handled the situation appropriately. She avoided a confrontation, did not demean the questioner, and steered the discussion back to the topic. Part of a presenter's responsibility is recognizing irrelevant questions and comments, and keeping control of the discussion.

> *He who trims himself to suit everyone will soon whittle himself away.*
>
> —Raymond Hull, playwright

Think of some strategies that a speaker could use to defuse a hostile questioner.

_____

_____

_____

## DID YOU KNOW?

✧ Mind mapping is a technique developed by a British brain researcher in the 1970s. Instead of making a list, you write the main topic of your presentation in the center of the paper and draw branches extending from it to highlight key points.

✧ Drinking soft drinks before speaking causes sibilance, a hissing sound informing certain words, especially words with "s" beginnings and endings.

✧ A researched fact of presenting is that most people attending a presentation will remember no more than five key points.

# PRACTICE

1. Decide whether you would prefer to answer questions during or after a presentation. Write a two-paragraph essay defending your choice, and provide good supporting statements.

2. Search the Internet for pointers about how to respond to questions after a presentation. Combine the information you find with the ideas in this workshop, and create a poster entitled, "Top Ten Ways to Answer Questions" to display in your classroom.

3. Make a list of at least 10 things you can say to a questioner when you don't know the answer to his or her question. Keep the list with your presentation notes so that you can use them when the time comes.

## On the Net

If there's one profession where presenting information and answering questions go hand in hand, it's public relations. To learn more about this industry, go to:

http://www.prsa.org

http://www.instituteforpr.com

http://lamar.colostate.edu/~hallahan/j13pr.htm

# SUMMARY

➤ Your presentation isn't ready until you feel confident about taking questions from your audience.

➤ Each method for taking questions has advantages and disadvantages.

➤ Providing a structured environment for questions and dealing with unwelcome interruptions is your job as the presenter.

Grant is a salesperson for a company that leases heavy equipment such as bulldozers and cranes to construction firms. His supervisors have asked him to give a presentation to a group of representatives from various companies on how to finance the equipment.

About halfway through his presentation, someone in the audience asks Grant a complex question. Grant provides a thorough answer, taking 10 minutes from his presentation.

When he gets back on track, another question comes from the audience. This time, Grant doesn't know the answer. He fudges a reply, but it confuses another person in the back of the room, who tells Grant that he doesn't understand the explanation.

Flustered by so many surprise questions, Grant loses control of his presentation. He thought that he was prepared enough to explain everything during his talk, and had planned to spend only a few minutes at the end answering any lingering questions.

However, he underestimated the kinds of questions his audience might ask, and failed to notify the audience that he would address questions after the presentation.

## Got It Right

Gloria, a fundraiser for a nonprofit organization, is preparing a 90-minute presentation to an audience of potential financial donors.

Gloria knows she will face some tough questions. When preparing for her talk, she thinks about specific questions her audience might ask and develops thoughtful answers.

At the beginning of her talk, Gloria tells her audience that they are free to ask questions at any time but she would prefer it if they could wait until the end. After a smooth and thorough presentation, Gloria begins to field questions.

She makes sure to repeat the question each person asks before she answers. When a particular question stumps Gloria, she says, "That's a good question. I'll be sure to get back to you when I find an answer."

Gloria embraces the question and answer period with enthusiasm. She respects the importance of giving potential donors thorough answers, knowing that her job is to make a good impression for her organization.

1. Explain the importance of questions and discussions during presentations.

   _____

   _____

   _____

2. Describe how to anticipate and plan for questions.

   _____

   _____

   _____

3. Describe the advantages and disadvantages of talking with individuals after the presentation.

   _____

   _____

   _____

# PROJECTS

1. Watch two TV panel discussion programs (e.g., a Sunday morning news panel). Write a review of the techniques that the speakers used in responding to questions and comments. Create a multimedia slide show that compares the two formats and their methods.

2. With several partners, create a puppet show that demonstrates all the wrong ways to ask questions and respond to them after a presentation. Perform the puppet show for a group of young students to introduce them to the etiquette of Q & A sessions.

©2001 PhotoDisc, Inc.

## MAKING IT MEANINGFUL

An old brain teaser challenges you to describe a spiral staircase without using your hands. This puzzler recognizes that the transfer of information from a speaker to a listener requires using a variety of delivery techniques. Sound, sight, touch—even smell and taste—can enhance a message and make it easier for an audience to understand and remember. This workshop provides methods for enhancing your listeners' understanding during your presentation.

### That Does Not Compute

Rory Gallagher, a computer technician, was invited to speak to a group of secretaries about using the new, upgraded software that he had designed. Rory was brilliant with computers—an expert on everything from silicon chips to streaming video. He built computers from spare parts, and some said he could install a hard drive with his eyes closed.

Rory brought a computer to the presentation, which he set up on a table in front of the room. He began by talking about the capacities of the computer itself. He then went on to explain the difference between hardware and software. He finished by going on about the details of how and why he designed the software.

✓ **How did Rory's presentation fail to inform the audience?**

# TOOLS OF THE TRADE

## *Methods for Enhancing Learning*

When planning an informational presentation, you'll need know exactly what you want your listeners to learn. You'll also need to organize your information clearly and logically, and deliver it in a way that will leave an impression on your audience.

➤ **Analogies.** It's always useful to compare new knowledge to something the audience is already familiar with. For example, a speaker teaching an audience to program a CD player might say, "Programming this device is a lot like programming a VCR or a clock radio."

➤ **Mnemonic devices.** Sometimes new information is so specialized that it doesn't relate to old knowledge. That's when a mnemonic device, or memory aid, can be helpful. For example, a teacher can help his or her students remember the order of the spectrum by introducing "ROY G. BIV" (Red, Orange, Yellow, Green, Blue, Indigo, and Violet).

➤ **Novel or vivid examples.** Original, distinctive examples are powerful teaching aids. For example, a speaker who wanted to make a strong point about the pain of discrimination might only look at and take questions from audience members with brown eyes.

➤ **Senses.** When you utilize your audience's senses—hearing, sight, touch, taste, and smell—you're sending a direct message to their brains. Information that is supported by a sense experience is easier to comprehend and retain.

➤ **Demonstrations.** If your information requires steps or a complex process, it's good to show a step-by-step example of how it should be done.

➤ **Games.** Whether you use paper-and-pencil games or versions of popular television game shows, games reinforce lessons by giving your listeners mental challenges.

➤ **Simulations.** Exercises such as safety procedures or drills may be best explained by constructing a mock environment in which audience members participate as if the real situation was occurring.

## Key Ideas

★ **analogy**— comparison based on similarities between things

★ **mnemonic device**—a technique used to aid memory

★ **vivid**—characterized by striking clarity, distinctness, or truth to life

★ **novel**— new, original, different, or unusual

★ **simulation**— the reproduction of the essential features of something, to aid in study or training

*" A moment's insight is sometimes worth a life experience. "*

—Oliver Wendell Holmes, physician and poet

## Create Your Learning Space

Though you typically can't do anything about the size of your presentation area, there are some things you can do with the room set-up to aid audience understanding.

➤ Place visual aids where they can be seen clearly by everyone.

➤ If the room is large and the group is small, designate the front rows as the seating area.

➤ Rearrange the chairs to facilitate conversation if you plan to have audience discussion sessions.

➤ If the listeners are to take notes or do any other writing, provide them with tables or other writing surfaces.

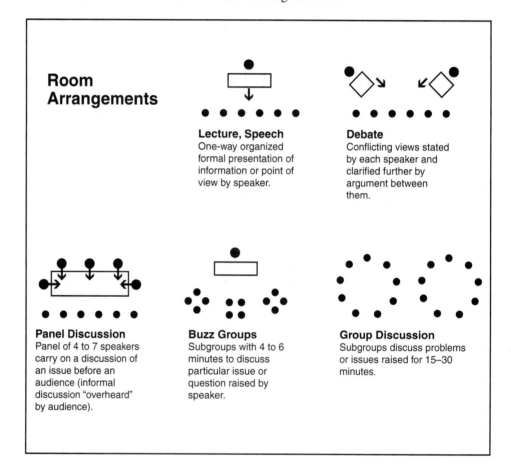

**Room Arrangements**

**Lecture, Speech**
One-way organized formal presentation of information or point of view by speaker.

**Debate**
Conflicting views stated by each speaker and clarified further by argument between them.

**Panel Discussion**
Panel of 4 to 7 speakers carry on a discussion of an issue before an audience (informal discussion "overheard" by audience).

**Buzz Groups**
Subgroups with 4 to 6 minutes to discuss particular issue or question raised by speaker.

**Group Discussion**
Subgroups discuss problems or issues raised for 15–30 minutes.

## DID YOU KNOW?

If listeners cannot relate new information that they already have, they won't learn. One dictionary definition of a *quetzal* is "a Central American trogon." This definition is meaningless if you don't know what a trogon is. (It's a parrot!)

# BASIC TRAINING

U.S. Army sergeants are in charge of training dozens of new recruits every year. Their responsibilities include teaching soldiers about Army routines, camp procedures, defense strategies, and, of course, discipline. To prepare for their leadership roles, sergeants must study training techniques. Because they know that not all recruits learn the same way, sergeants must use a variety of methods when planning training sessions.

Imagine that you're a sergeant in the U.S. Army. You've been asked to prepare training sessions for your new recruits on the following topics. For each topic, choose at least two methods for enhancing the informative session. Explain how you would use the teaching method in each instance.

1. Repairing Equipment in a Desert

2. Treating Military Supervisors Respectfully

3. Shining Your Belts and Shoes

4. Teamwork

5. Setting Up a Tent

| | TOPIC 1 | TOPIC 2 | TOPIC 3 | TOPIC 4 | TOPIC 5 |
|---|---|---|---|---|---|
| Analogies | | | | | |
| Mnemonic devices | | | | | |
| Novel or vivid examples | | | | | |
| Senses | | | | | |
| Demonstrations | | | | | |
| Games | | | | | |
| Simulations | | | | | |

## *Please Take a Seat*

Ramón Garcia is one of those lucky people who isn't at all nervous about speaking to large groups. He enjoys it!

Ramón's supervisor asked him to speak on the use of the company's new security system. Ramón read all that he could, checked the Web site of the company that makes the security system, and even called the manufacturer for more data.

Ramón wanted to be well prepared, and he also wanted his audience to be comfortable. He planned the room arrangement in two segments. He placed the television and the lectern at the front of the room for his formal explanation.

In the second segment, the participants would brainstorm, and afterward Ramón would write their ideas on a flip chart at the front of the room.

Ramón combined a well-planned lecture with small-group discussion and brainstorming. This allowed the people in the audience to benefit from relating ideas to previous knowledge, sharing ideas, and asking questions in a comfortable setting.

Draw a diagram of ideal room arrangements for each segment of Ramón's presentation.

| Segment 1 | Segment 2 |
| --- | --- |
|  |  |

## PRACTICE

1.  How could you engage more than one sense in each of the following presentations?

    Preparing Income Tax Returns _____

    The Latest Hairstyling Tips _____

    Baking Chocolate Chip Cookies _____

    Saving Lives with CPR _____

    Music Production Companies _____

    Pet Grooming for Profit _____

2.  If you were making a presentation to a group of senior citizens about new electronic banking practices, how would you relate the new ideas to knowledge they already have? Give a few examples of useful analogies.

3.  With a partner, check several Internet sites for information about presentation room arrangements. Draw a diagram of an arrangement, and give an explanation of why it is most appropriate for a specific kind of presentation.

## SUMMARY

➤ When planning an informational presentation, you'll need to organize your information clearly and logically, and deliver it in a way that will leave an impression on your audience.

➤ It's always useful to compare new knowledge to something the audience is already familiar with.

➤ Novel or vivid examples are powerful teaching aids.

➤ Information that is supported by a sensory experience is easier to comprehend and retain.

➤ Though you typically can't do anything about the size of your presentation area, you can set-up your room to aid audience understanding.

1. How can a presenter prepare to make his or her remarks meaningful to an audience?

_____

_____

_____

2. Why are analogies important when introducing unfamiliar content?

_____

_____

_____

3. Why do novel and vivid presentations help maintain audience interest?

_____

_____

_____

4. What should you do when you're presenting to a small group in a large room?

_____

_____

_____

> *The best way to sound like you know what you're talking about is to know what you're talking about.*
>
> —Anonymous

# PROJECTS

1. Attend a presentation and observe how effectively the presenter uses analogies, mnemonics, and novelty to increase learning and audience attention. Write a critique of the presentation, relating each of the three areas and explaining the reasons for your evaluation.

2. Imagine that you are selected to plan a conference for 100 firefighters in your community. Design four room arrangements for the following conference schedule:

   **Part 1.** Keynote address to a group of 100 firefighters.

   **Part 2.** Break-out sessions in which groups of 20 firefighters attend learning demonstrations performed by their peers.

   **Part 3.** Panel discussion in which 5 firefighters address groups of 10 participants, discussing problems and concerns raised in Part 2.

   **Part 4.** Interview session in which the keynote speaker fields questions from the fire chief while the audience observes.

3. Analogies are effective only if the listener understands the comparison. Read several articles in *Time* or *Newsweek*, and highlight all the analogies that you find. Using a T-chart, list the analogies on the left and their explanations on the right. If there are any analogies that you do not understand, note them and research their meanings.

*If your information requires steps or a complex process, it's good to show a step-by-step example of how it should be done.*

©2001 PhotoDisc, Inc.

71

## GOALS

➥ Learn how skilled communicators capture the attention of an audience.

➥ Understand the strategies of persuasive speaking.

©2001 PhotoDisc, Inc.

## POWERFUL PRESENTERS

Ask your friends, teachers, or relatives to name a talented public speaker. Chances are that you'll hear one of these names: John F. Kennedy, Martin Luther King, Jr., Jesse Jackson, Franklin Delano Roosevelt, Madeleine Albright, or Billy Graham. These religious and political leaders have had the power to engage their listeners and stir them to action. This workshop will show you how to enhance your speaking skills and to use your powers of persuasion in the workplace.

### Sharing the Dream

On August 28, 1963, Dr. Martin Luther King, Jr. delivered his famous "I Have a Dream" speech on the steps of the Capitol building in Washington, D.C. Decades later, this speech is still memorized by school children, repeated by civic leaders, and studied by scholars. The words of that speech had a powerful effect on Dr. King's listeners. The images he used provoked emotions that caused people to work harder for the cause of civil rights.

The power of Dr. King's speech came from both content and delivery. His words had deep meaning, and the passion with which he spoke encouraged people from all parts of the country to become involved with his cause. Dr. King's persuasive talents were never more forceful than on that day in August.

✔ *Why are both content and delivery important in a persuasive speech?*

# TOOLS OF THE TRADE

## Three Types of Persuasion

In business, most persuasive presentations are made to relatively small groups. They might be delivered by vendors at department meetings, company conventions, trade shows, or conferences. The most common purposes of persuasive presentations are to convince others to buy your product or service, to influence listeners to allocate budget dollars or resources to a project or cause, or to propose a new idea or a change in process or procedure. Three main types of persuasion follow.

➤ **Fact**—getting your listeners to accept facts as presented

➤ **Value**—justifying your opinion about certain values

➤ **Action**—persuading your listeners to take a specific course of action

In a sales presentation, all three of these come into play.

➤ First, the speaker talks persuasively about the features of a product or service (**fact**).

➤ Next, the speaker tries to convince the audience that his or her product or service is better than any other (**value**).

➤ Finally, the speaker tries to persuade the audience to buy the product or service (**action**).

> ## Key Ideas
>
> ★ **persuasive**—having the power to convince someone to do or believe something
>
> ★ **imagery**—the use of vivid or figurative language to emphasize a quality
>
> ★ **repetition**—the act or process of saying or writing something repeatedly

## Why Should They Want What You Have?

When you are trying to sell a product or service, it's important to explain how that product or service benefits your customer. Remember to point out the features and benefits of buying your product or service.

➤ **Features**—part of the product's built-in design, such as the sunroof of a car.

➤ **Benefits**—what the product will do for the consumer, such as saving money on bills or helping the environment.

## Responding to the Audience

If you hope to persuade your audience, you'll need to reach the core of their emotions. Reading the body language of your audience will tell you how well your message is getting through.

➤ **Confusion.** Listeners may send nonverbal cues, such as pursed lips, tilting of the head, raised eyebrows. Review what you've said, and say it in a different way. You might also stop and ask for questions.

➤ **Indifference.** Listeners slouch or fidget. Stop and ask for questions that concern the audience's needs and interests.

73

## Making Words Come Alive

Imagery is not only used in poetry. Many successful public speakers use imagery and repetition in their presentations to persuade audiences and stir emotions. When speakers are able to reach the hearts of the audience as well as their minds, they are better able to persuade the listeners to take action.

➤ **Imagery.** By using descriptive words, speakers enable listeners to mentally picture what is being said. For example, in his "I Have a Dream" speech, Dr. Martin Luther King, Jr. used vivid words to paint a picture of what life was like for black Americans in 1963.

*"Some of you have come fresh from narrow cells. Some of you have come from areas where your quest for freedom left you battered by the storms of persecution and staggered by the winds of police brutality."*

➤ **Repetition.** Repeating a sentence or phrase is an effective way to imprint the minds and memory of your audience. For example, President Franklin D. Roosevelt, in his 1937 inaugural address, repetitively used the phrase "I see":

*"I see millions whose daily lives in city and on farm continue under conditions labeled indecent . . . I see millions denied education . . . I see millions lacking the means to buy the products of farm and factory . . ."*

## Delivering Your Message

Delivering your presentation with ease and without distraction will help your audience gain meaning from your words.

➤ **Notes and eye contact.** Do not read form your notes. Use them only for brief reference, and keep your eyes on your audience.

➤ **Gestures.** Use meaningful movements and gestures to make your points, but don't draw attention to them. Avoid distracting movements, such as pacing, or playing with your glasses or jewelry.

➤ **Smile.** Smiling will help you and your audience feel at ease.

➤ **Voice.** To ensure that you will be heard, send your voice out to the person who is at the greatest distance form you. Speak confidently and at a normal pace.

## Persuasive Presentation Steps

The following steps are an effective formula for delivering a persuasive speech.

1. Gain the audience's attention.
2. Identify a need the audience has.
3. Propose your solution, idea, or product that meets that need.
4. Use supporting details to explain how your solution meets that need.
5. Call for action. Motivate the audience to put your solution into effect (buy your product, make a change, etc.).

# THE BLOOD DRIVE: PERSUASION TECHNIQUES

## Segment 6

Sam is about to make a blood drive presentation. This time, however, you're the audience. Sam will try to persuade you to do something that 95 percent of people don't do—donate blood. As you watch Sam's presentation, evaluate the arguments and facts he uses to persuade you. Does Sam successfully overcome your objections? Are you ready to roll up your sleeves?

*Sam explains the importance of donating blood.*

## Post-Viewing Questions

**1.** What arguments and facts did Sam use to persuade you?

_____

_____

_____

**2.** How did he try to overcome any objections you might have? How well did he do?

_____

_____

_____

75

## *"Ain't I a Woman?"*

In December 1851, Sojourner Truth, an African American champion of women's rights, spoke at a women's convention in Akron, Ohio. She wanted her audience to understand that the speeches of male legislators who pretended to have the interests of women in mind, when they refused to allow them to vote, were simply empty words. They were hollow promises meant to keep females "in their place."

Pointing to a politician, Sojourner Truth said, "That man over there says that women need to be helped into carriages, and lifted over ditches, and to have best place everywhere. Nobody ever helps me into carriages, or over mud-puddles, or gives me any best place! And ain't I a woman?"

With this simple statement, Sojourner Truth pointed out the politicians' hypocrisy. Her emotional speech, filled with images and the repeated phrase "Ain't I a woman?" moved her listeners to take action against slavery and the oppression of women.

Repetition is a convincing device used in persuasive speaking. Repeated phrases stick with listeners. Advertisers know this. That's why they create musical jingles that people hum, often remembering them for years.

List some advertising slogans or phrases that you recall.

_____

_____

What images do the slogans bring to your mind? How do they use repetition?

_____

_____

*You can have the most wonderful product in the world, but if people don't know about it, it's not going to be worth much . . . you need to generate interest, and you need to create excitement.*

—Donald Trump

# PRACTICE

1. Use the Internet or other resources to find examples of persuasive speeches. Download and print several, and highlight examples of imagery and repetition in each. Engage other students in a discussion about the effectiveness of these techniques in speeches.

2. With a partner, write two persuasive speeches about the same topic. One should contain imagery and repetition; the other should not. Present each speech to the class for evaluation.

3. Read a newspaper or magazine advertisement for a product or service. Write and deliver a two-minute persuasive speech to sell the product.

©2001 PhotoDisc, Inc.

*If you hope to persuade your audience, you'll need to reach the core of their emotions.*

# SUMMARY

➤ The most common purposes of persuasive presentations are to convince others to buy your product or service, to influence listeners to allocate budget dollars or resources to a project or cause, or to propose a new idea or a change in process or procedure.

➤ Skilled persuasive speakers use imagery and repetition.

➤ Persuasive presentations should recognize the needs of the audience.

## The Evils of Persuasion: Adolf Hitler and the Nazi Party

Adolph Hitler, founder of the Nazi Party, was one of the most persuasive speakers and possibly the most dangerous man that has
ever existed. Often called the "Devil's Miracle Man," Hitler used
persuasive speaking and propaganda to prey upon the vulnerability of the German people.
He ultimately convinced the nation of Germany to adopt the philosophy of the Nazi Party,
a murderous political group that took over six million lives between 1933 and 1945.

Hitler's hatred for all ethnic and racial groups outside of the Aryan race, especially the
Jews, began in October of 1907. He read the books of anti-Jewish theorists and developed
a belief that Jewish people continued to undermine the German nation and the purity of
the Aryan race. He became convinced that fate had chosen him to rescue Germany from
the shackles of the Bolsheviks and Jews, and he began to speak out against these groups.

Unfortunately, people listened and even began to agree with him. How did Hitler do
this? Why did so many believe in his evil ways and follow the wishes of a cruel and scary
mastermind?

Adolph Hitler had a charismatic character and was a powerful orator. His speeches were
emotional and captivating. He made the German people believe that he felt their pain
and presented his beliefs as the only solution. He grasped people's attention and was
passionate about his topic. An American journalist once commented, "When, at the
climax of a speech, he sways from one side to the other, his listeners sway with him;
when he leans forward and (ends the speech), they are either awed and silent or on their
feet in a frenzy."

It has been said that the Nazis rose to power on the empty stomachs of the German
people. Hitler took advantage of a hurting audience. Germany was suffering from a
post-war depression. Unemployment was high, illness was sweeping the nation, and
many people were starving.

Using the vulnerability of the German people and exercising his strong oratory skills,
Hitler identified the enemies of Germany. Anyone who was non-Aryan, including Jews,
Bolsheviks, and even communists, were described by Hitler as "devils." According to Hitler,
those groups were responsible for the social, political, and economic troubles of Germany.
Sadly, people listened and believed, making Jews and others the scapegoats for all of
Germany's problems.

# REVIEW QUESTIONS

1. List and describe three types of persuasion typically used in business presentations.

   _____

   _____

2. Describe some strategies used in persuasive presentations.

   _____

   _____

3. Define imagery and repetition, and explain how speakers use these methods to persuade audiences.

   _____

   _____

# PROJECTS

1. Watch an infomercial on television, and analyze its persuasive strategies. Make a list of the techniques you observed, as well as a second list of strategies that were not used. Write a short review of the program, suggesting how it might be improved.

2. Using the Internet or the local library, find some examples of recorded speeches. Listen to each just once, without taking any notes. At the end of each speech, write down its major points. Then listen to it again. Did you pick up the main ideas? What parts of the speech were the most memorable? Did imagery or repetition help you remember the main ideas? Create transparencies or slides to use in reporting your findings to your class.

3. To test the effectiveness of slogans, cut some out of old magazine ads. Then tape or glue each to a card, and write the name of the company on the back. Display each ad to members of your class, one at a time. Record how many of the slogans they can identify. Create a graph that demonstrates your results.

This guide has provided pointers about how to make compelling presentations on the job. You have learned to identify the needs and interests of your audience, how to gather and organize content, how to use visual aids, and how to overcome the fear of public speaking. Now, it's time to apply the strategies you've learned to create a masterful presentation with a minimum of stress.

Working in teams, contact a local Rotary or Kiwanis Club, a Chamber of Commerce or school board, the City Council, or a local Toastmasters chapter. Ask to be placed on their agenda to make a presentation to their members.

1. Choose a topic that meets the needs and interests of your audience. Develop an audience profile by talking with the leader of the organization.

2. Prior to giving your presentation, ask the leader of the organization if you can visit the room you will be speaking in. Create a diagram of the room arrangement on the following worksheet.

3. Use the K-W-L reading and research strategy to read and learn about your topic. Keep a list of the resources you are using and make sure the sources are reliable and related to your topic. Ask yourself, "What am I trying to convey to my audience?"

4. Organize and outline your ideas, using the following worksheet as a guide. (You may have more or fewer key ideas and subtopics. Be sure to keep key ideas at a maximum of five.) Create note cards with one main idea written on each card.

5. Write four possible introductions and four possible conclusions for your presentation. Decide amongst your team which ones to use.

6. Plan and create at least three visual aids to enhance your presentation (graphs, charts, tables, diagrams, photos, audio, video, etc.).

7. Create a list of 10 possible questions your audience might ask during or after your presentation. Then, create answers for each of those questions.

8. Rehearse your presentation aloud. It should be about five minutes in length. Get feedback from your team about ways to improve your delivery. Don't forget to do some breathing and relaxation exercises before the big day!

# WORKSHEET 1: YOUR AUDIENCE

## *Audience Profile*

Age ranges _____

Level of education _____

Race/sex _____

Interests or hobbies _____

Level of knowledge about your topic _____

Occupations _____

Disabilities _____

Native languages _____

## *Room Arrangement*

# WORKSHEET 2: YOUR TOPIC

## K-W-L Strategy

TOPIC: _____

| BEFORE RESEARCH<br>What do I know<br>about the topic? | BEFORE RESEARCH<br>What do I want<br>to learn? | AFTER RESEARCH<br>What have<br>I learned? |
|---|---|---|
|  |  |  |

## Topic Outline

Introduction _____

Key Idea #1 _____

    Subtopic #1 _____

    Subtopic #2 _____

    Subtopic #3 _____

Transition _____

Key Idea #2 _____

    Subtopic #1 _____

    Subtopic #2 _____

    Subtopic #3 _____

Transition _____

Key Idea #3 _____

    Subtopic #1 _____

    Subtopic #2 _____

    Subtopic #3 _____

Conclusion _____

# WORKSHEET 3: Q & A

## *Anticipated Questions and Answers*

1._____

_____

Answer: _____

2._____

_____

Answer: _____

3._____

_____

Answer: _____

4._____

_____

Answer: _____

5._____

_____

Answer: _____

6._____

_____

Answer: _____

7._____

_____

Answer: _____

8._____

_____

Answer: _____

9._____

_____

Answer: _____

10._____

_____

Answer: _____

# GLOSSARY

## A

**analogy**—comparison based on similarities between things

**anecdote**—a brief story that is amusing, interesting, or personal

**anxiety**—mental uneasiness, usually having to do with some anticipated event

**apprehension**—fear of some future event

**audience**—a reading, viewing, or listening public

## B

**barrier**—an obstacle; something that stands in the way

## C

**causal**—related to causes and effects

**chronological**—the order in which events should or did occur, from first event to last event

**clarity**—clearness; lack of confusion

**communication**—an ongoing, two-way process in which a sender conveys a message and a receiver attaches meaning to it

## D

**defuse**—to calm or pacify; to make less threatening or dangerous

**demographics**—statistical characteristics of human populations

## E

**encore**—an additional or repeated performance of something in response to a demand from an audience

**environment**—setting, surroundings

**evidence**—examples and data that support an idea

## G

**graphic**—a visual device, such as a chart, a photo, or a map that is used to illustrate information

## I

**imagery**—the use of vivid or figurative language to emphasize a quality

**inform**—to share information with others

**irrelevant**—not applicable or important

## L

**long-winded**—using too many words

## M

**mnemonic device**—a technique used to aid memory

## N

**networking**—getting referred to the people you don't know through the people you do know; connecting with people or groups who can assist you in finding a job

**nonverbal communication**—gestures, facial expressions, movements, body language, and tones of voice that convey a feeling, attitude, or message

**novel**—new, original, different, or unusual

## O

**oral presentation**—a speech given to a group of people

## P

**persuade**—to convince others to accept your ideas or to act in a certain way

**persuasive**—having the power to convince someone to do or believe something

**physiological**—having to do with physical characteristics

**profile**—a description of a group of people, including their demographics, interests, and concerns

**psychological**—having to do with mental characteristics

**purpose**—intention

## Q

**Q & A**—abbreviation commonly used for "question and answer"

## R

**reliable**—from a source that can be counted on for accuracy

**repetition**—the act or process of saying or writing something repeatedly

**rhetorical question**—a question that does not expect an answer

## S

**simulation**—the reproduction of the essential features of something, to aid in study or training

**spatial**—according to location

**stereotype**—an oversimplified, prejudiced attitude toward certain groups of people held by other groups of people

## T

**topical**—according to topic

**transition**—a shift or progression from one thing to another

**transparency**—a sheet of plastic used to show images with a projector

## V

**value**—to have a high regard for someone or something

**verbal communication**—the exchange of information or ideas through spoken or written words

**visual aid**—something such as a model, chart, or movie that is used as a complement to a lesson or presentation

**vivid**—characterized by striking clarity, distinctness, or truth to life

# NOTES